EARLY CHILDHOOD EDUCATION SERIES

Leslie R. Williams, Editor

ADVISORY BOARD: Barbara T. Bowman, Harriet K. Cuffaro, Stephanie Feeney,
Doris Pronin Fromberg, Celia Genishi, Stacie G. Goffin, Dominic F. Gullo,
Alice Sterling Honig, Elizabeth Jones, Gwen Morgan, David Weikart

(Continued)

the COLORS *of learning*

INTEGRATING THE VISUAL ARTS INTO THE EARLY CHILDHOOD CURRICULUM

Rosemary Althouse
Margaret H. Johnson
Sharon T. Mitchell

Foreword by Carol Seefeldt

TEACHERS COLLEGE PRESS

Teachers College
Columbia University
New York and London

naeyc

National Association
for the Education of
Young Children

Published simultaneously by Teachers College Press, 1234 Amsterdam Avenue, New York, NY 10027 and the National Association for the Education of Young Children, 1509 16th Street NW, Washington, DC 20036-1426

Library of Congress Cataloging-in-Publication Data

Althouse, Rosemary, 1932–
    The colors of learning : integrating the visual arts into the early childhood curriculum / Rosemary Althouse, Margaret H. Johnson, Sharon T. Mitchell.
        p. cm. — (Early childhood education series)
    ISBN 0-8077-4274-0 (pbk.)
    1. Art—Study and teaching (Early childhood)   I. Johnson, Margaret H.   II. Mitchell, Sharon T.   III. Title.   IV. Early childhood education series (Teachers College Press)
LB1139.5.A78 A48 2002
372.5'044—dc21   2002072232

ISBN 0-8077-4274-0 (paper)

NAEYC item 215

Printed on acid-free paper

Manufactured in the United States of America

13 12 11   8 7 6 5 4

In memory of Julia Schwartz and Nancy Douglas,
whose joint influence brought us together

In honor of Marguerite (Peg) Cowan, Louise Beltramo,
and Betty Lou Land, whose teaching inspired us

In recognition of the children and teachers who continue
to be our instructors

Contents

Foreword

Integral to life itself, art is also an integral part of all education. Especially during the early years of life, art, another language for learning, is a critical part of the curriculum in all good schools for young children. Nevertheless, the role of the visual arts in today's early childhood curriculum is ambiguous.

Under pressure to account for early childhood methods and practices and to prepare young children to succeed in an increasingly academic educational world, far too many early childhood teachers have misinterpreted the role of the visual arts in children's learning. With the current focus on early literacy skills and political forces promoting the development of phonemic awareness as the only essential skill to be gained during the early years, the visual arts are far too often viewed as a frill, something to do when "real work" has been completed. Or, not understanding the true meaning and value of the visual arts, others think of art as an appropriate way for children to relax, mess around, and give full reign to their emotions. And then there are those educators who do want to include the visual arts in the curriculum, but unclear of the philosophy, research, and theory of art as a cognitive skill, provide children with cute things to cut, paste, or copy.

For years early childhood educators have longed for information on the theory, research, and practice of art in the early childhood program. *The Colors of Learning: Integrating the Visual Arts into the Early Childhood Curriculum* gives teachers knowledge of the visual arts that will enable them to develop new, accurate understanding of the visual arts as another mode of learning.

Dewey's (1934/1980) philosophy of art as experience provides the foundation for understanding the role of the teacher in the visual arts. This role involves teacher and children in joint meaningful experiences that call for observing, questioning, discussing, and finding out, and the time and opportunity for reflection.

The teacher is active. It is the teacher who plans and provides actual, real, and intensely meaningful experiences for children; who provides and arranges the appropriate materials for children; who guides their art by introducing new ideas through literature; who talks to children about their art; who pushes children to think anew, to question, to find other ways of using materials, or to extend an experience.

Children are active. Given meaningful experiences, children express their own individual feelings, ideas, and reflections through the visual arts.

With a background of experiences and appropriate motivating materials, children are put in charge. They are the ones who must search their memories of an experience, think of symbols to represent their ideas, and then find ways to transcribe these symbols to paper. Throughout, children are the ones who are setting goals for themselves, planning ways to achieve these, monitoring their progress, and changing ideas and methods that did not work and selecting other methods to continue. In the end, the children are the ones who experience the joy, the thrill, and the pleasure of achieving their goals.

Vygotsky's theories offer the early childhood educator insights into how children's thinking processes and academic growth are integrated through the visual arts. The role of the teacher in promoting children's art work is clarified. How teachers talk to children about their art, introduce new vocabulary, and help children reflect and talk about their own art and the art of others is clearly illustrated in *The Colors of Learning*. The practical examples and illustrations given will enable the early childhood educator to develop the skills of scaffolding children's learning, not just in the visual arts, but throughout the curriculum.

Those of us who believe that learning is a process of constructing and reconstructing and that the emphasis should be placed on how children think as well as what they think about, will find this book an organizing force. *The Colors of Learning* bridges the gap between Dewey's philosophy of art, Vygotskian ideas of teaching, and the actual practice of the visual arts. Rosemary Althouse, Margaret Johnson, and Sharon Mitchell who guided a team of early childhood educators and art specialists to create *The Colors of Learning*, have given the field of early education a valuable, useable gift—one that will have a great impact on young children's lives and those who teach them.

—*Carol Seefeldt*

Preface

We hold a strong conviction that young children will benefit from having art experiences as an integrated part of the curriculum. We want this book to help early childhood educators use children's language, actions, interests, and discoveries as the basis for planning their art experiences. We also want to help early childhood educators develop and implement more effective language as they talk with children about their art work—what we call "art talk."

In this book we utilize a consensus of beliefs about what constitutes developmentally appropriate practices in the visual arts. These beliefs are drawn from statements endorsed by the National Association for the Education of Young Children (NAEYC) and the National Art Education Association (NAEA). These practices include providing children with daily opportunities for aesthetic expression and appreciation in the arts by encouraging their experimentation with a variety of developmentally appropriate art media, art forms, and art processes (Bredekamp & Copple, 1997).

The content for this book developed out of a 3-year study we conducted with five early childhood teachers. In carrying out our study—and writing this book—we have respected each other's differences and recognized that each of us had a vital contribution to make. We are all educators. Two of us are university professors, Rosemary in early childhood and Margaret in art and design. Sharon is a public school teacher of 4-year-old children. While each of us has her own area of expertise, we all share the same philosophy of education. We believe that children construct and reconstruct their own learning as they interact with their environment. This constructivist point of view places as much importance on *how* children think as on *what* they think.

We chose classroom teachers for our study whose experiential backgrounds and present teaching methods were congruent with ours. Teachers and investigators met initially to discuss the study. We visited preschools, kindergartens, and elementary schools that had adapted the Reggio Emilia approach to early childhood education. We found that many aspects of the Reggio Emilia practices (Cadwell, 1997; Edwards, Gandini, & Forman, 1998) corresponded with our philosophy and purposes.

During the study we met periodically to discuss how the children were progressing, which techniques were most successful, and when modifications should be made. Student portfolios were maintained as documents for evaluation using the Art Portfolio Assessment Scale (see Appendix A).

Children's verbal and artistic expressions were documented through teachers' notes, videotapes, and the Art Talk Checklist (see Appendix B). These data were analyzed to inform us about children's actions with media and interactions with teachers and peers, and the development and implementation of effective instructional strategies.

The stories we tell in this book come from the classrooms in our study, but the names of the teachers and children have been changed. The teachers in our study learned more about their children and art than they had expected. We learned the most of all. There were many surprises for all of us as we observed the children's ability to develop with guidance and to plan and to execute their plans as they worked with art media. We saw the value of integrating art into the early childhood curriculum.

We begin our book with its theoretical underpinnings in Chapter 1, including a discussion of Vygotsky's theories of language and social interaction. We look at historical and current conceptions about integrating visual art into the early childhood curriculum. Chapter 2 presents aspects of the young child's classroom environment that teachers can use to promote this integration. Art media, tools, the introduction of learning areas, and technology are the focus of Chapter 3. We emphasize that visual art materials should be readily available and that technology is a valuable tool in fostering artistic expression.

In Chapter 4, we help teachers learn about guiding children as they explore and create with art media. Chapter 5 shows teachers how language can be used effectively to build children's conceptual knowledge and guide them in their art making. In Chapter 6, we focus on introducing young children to artists, as they learn to see themselves as artists.

Chapter 7 provides early childhood teachers with ideas to involve parents and to collaborate with art specialists in planning art experiences for their students. Chapter 8 presents reflections from the teachers and administrators who were involved in the making of this book. Finally, for teachers who want to deepen their understanding of art concepts and may not have art specialists in their schools, the appendices provide additional information about children's art development and the language of art.

We invite teachers of young children to join us in planning art activities that can be integrated into the early childhood curriculum and in using art language with art making to improve children's artistic thinking and learning.

Acknowledgments

The authors wish to thank Winthrop University, its Richard W. Riley College of Education, and the Department of Art and Design within its College of Visual and Performing Arts for their cooperation in this study. We are indebted to several teachers in the Rock Hill, South Carolina, School District who inspired us. They are Mia Beleos, third-grade teacher at Lesslie Elementary School; Tracy Craven, first-grade teacher at Oakdale Elementary School; Lynn LeGrand, second-grade teacher at Rosewood Elementary School; and Mary Watson, kindergarten teacher at Macfeat Early Childhood Laboratory School, Winthrop University.

We were fortunate to have two art specialists work with us and the teachers. They are Rebecca Ramsey at Oakdale Elementary School and Diane English at Lesslie Elementary School.

We wish to thank Stephen Ward, Principal of Rosewood Elementary School; Larry Doggett, Principal of Oakdale Elementary School; Barbara Beam, Principal of Lesslie Elementary School; and Ruth Greer, Director of the Macfeat Early Childhood Laboratory School at Winthrop University.

We express our appreciation to Chad Dresbach, professor of Art and Design at Winthrop University, for his help with the photographs and to *The Herald* (Rock Hill) for permission to include one of their photographs in this book. We appreciate the hospitality of Peggy Rivers, practicing artist and art professor at Gaston College in North Carolina. She showed us her paintings in the Winthrop Gallery, and we visited her studio at the Center for the Arts in Rock Hill.

Finally, we thank Susan Liddicoat of Teachers College Press for her wise advice, kind patience, and continuing support of our project throughout the editing phase of the process.

1 Integrating Art into the Early Childhood Curriculum

Two third-grade children were discussing what they knew about fish. Charlotte showed Mitchell a labeled diagram of a fish, which she had copied from the chalkboard in Mrs. Beam's classroom. She proudly read the words under each labeled part of the fish. Mitchell listened carefully and then showed Charlotte the fish he had drawn in his classroom.

Charlotte: Your picture isn't clear and you don't know the names of the parts of the fish. It looks very "swimmy." And you didn't label its parts.

Mitchell: It looks swimmy because I used watercolor to show it swimming in the water, and I can too name the parts! (*He proudly pointed out the parts of the fish in his painting and named them.*)

Charlotte: (*surprised*) How did you know that?

Mitchell: Mr. Glenn asked our class to look at our real goldfish in the aquarium and talk about their parts. Then we could use any art materials to make a fish. Mine was funny looking, and it kept swimming around. So I looked on the Internet and in the books in our resource center. That's how I learned the names of the parts!

Charlotte: We didn't do that in my classroom. We just copied the chart on the board. I think your fish is pretty with all its colors.

The children in this classroom scenario had very different learning experiences. Mitchell's teacher valued the integrated curriculum. Mitchell's teacher asked his students to examine the goldfish in the aquarium over a period of time, and to take notes and make sketches of them. He suggested that his students use the Internet, their science books, and books about fish from the library to learn about the fish, and he encouraged them to talk with each other about the parts of the goldfish. Charlotte's teacher taught a more traditional curriculum.

The integrated curriculum can be thought of as a way to unite all subject matter and content from separate disciplines into a whole. According to NAEYC, an integrated approach to teaching and learning exists when curriculum goals address learning in all developmental areas: physical, social, emotional, language, aesthetic, and intellectual (Bredekamp & Copple, 1997, p. 130).

Consistent with a focus on the integrated curriculum, Gardner's theory of multiple intelligences (1983) offers an expanded vision of the possibilities of learning, beyond the traditional emphasis in schools on the linguistic and logico-mathematical domains. The arts are being recognized for their potential to provide significant learning. Eisner (1990), among many contemporary art educators, has pointed out that a more comprehensive view of knowledge includes the arts, in which we "recognize that the avenues to human understanding exceed, widely exceed, what it is that can be said through science alone" (p. 34). Through the arts, children can be given opportunities to express their evolving concepts and constructed understandings about their world and their experiences.

The professional associations of both early childhood and visual arts educators, NAEYC and NAEA, underscore the importance of the arts in the early childhood curriculum. In NAEYC's *Developmentally Appropriate Practice in Early Childhood Programs* (Bredekamp & Copple, 1997), a section entitled "Examples of Appropriate and Inappropriate Practices for 3- through 5-Year-Olds" states:

> Children have daily opportunities for aesthetic expression and appreciation through art and music. Children experiment and enjoy various forms of dramatic play, music and dance. A variety of art media, such as markers, crayons, paints and clay, are available for creative expression and representation of ideas and feelings. (p. 132)

At the 6- through 8-year-old level, it is recommended that

> art, music, drama, dance, and other arts are the explicit focus of children's study at times. On other occasions, when relevant, the fine arts are integrated into other areas of the curriculum, such as social studies or mathematics. Children are encouraged to express themselves physically and aesthetically, represent ideas and feelings, and acquire fundamental concepts and skills in the fine arts. (p. 174)

The National Visual Arts Standards (NAEA, 1995) state:

> As they move from kindergarten through the early grades, students develop skills of observation, and they learn to examine the objects and events of their lives. At the same time, they grow in ability to describe, interpret, evaluate, and respond to work in the visual arts. (p. 15)

Beyond learning *about* art through art instruction, in an integrated approach in early childhood classrooms students are given an opportunity to learn *through* art in the context of their learning in other areas of the classroom curriculum. Examples of integrating visual art by connecting learning in art to learning in other areas of the curriculum are presented throughout this book: in language arts, social studies, science, and mathematics. As Simpson and her coauthors (1998) write, "Art becomes part of the real world and understood as an integral piece of the human condition. . . . Concepts experienced across disciplines are strongly connected to the learner" (p. 317). Goldberg (1997) sees the arts as "teaching methodologies," whereby students actively work with a knowledge base as they construct their understandings through an art form, "creating a personal connection to the subject matter" (p. 3).

We, as most early childhood and art educators, support a cognitive theory in visual arts education, in which art is considered a language to communicate ideas and feelings (Engle, 1995; Gardner, 1990; Seefeldt, 1995). Our constructivist perspective supports a view of cognitive development in which children create individual meanings and understandings of their experiences in art through their interactions with art media and art language (Burton, 1980a, 1980b; Slavin, 1994; Vygotsky, 1962).

RELEVANCY OF VYGOTSKY'S THEORIES OF LANGUAGE AND SOCIAL INTERACTION

The learning theory of Lev Vygotsky (1962), with its emphasis on socially shared interaction, provides a framework for implementing an integrated approach to learning. Vygotsky believed that language plays a central role in mental development. By responding to children's questions and guiding their research, teachers utilizing an integrated curriculum can promote children's higher order thinking. Young children often communicate through drawing, including their scribbling. Integrating art into the curriculum fosters children's use of symbols to communicate and express their ideas and feelings. For many years, art education research has supported the proposition that guided discussions with children related to artistic perception and process produce positive gains in verbalization as well as in artistic production (Bradley, 1968; Cromer, 1975; Douglas & Schwartz, 1967; Hogg & McWhinnie, 1968; Wilson, 1966).

Developmental psychologists have long emphasized the role of society in the child's development, as in Jerome Bruner's (1966) account of the development of human communication. Although Piaget stressed manipulation of objects, he believed that social interaction was necessary in learning (Wadsworth, 1966). It is through social interaction that children learn that other children have ideas different from their own.

The work of Piaget has been influential in defining the role of adults and peers in children's learning. Piaget believed that children construct their own knowledge as they interact with their environment according to the state of readiness of their mental schemata or already existing concepts (DeVries & Kohlberg, 1987). He felt that maturation alone does not determine development and that children profited from sharing experiences with adults and other children, especially through language (Bodrova & Leong, 1996).

According to Vygotsky, both receptive and expressive language have their origins in the social and cultural experiences of children. He also believed that in infancy and up to about age 2, language was not essential to thinking. This is in line with Piaget's belief that, in the beginning, thought precedes language. Vygotsky maintained that children often think better when they talk to themselves. Verbalization helps them to attend to and complete a task. This private verbal speech becomes less audible as children mature (Berk & Winsler, 1995).

There are many ways teachers can help children reflect on their own thinking. One way is to ask them to write or draw their understanding of an experience or an idea. For example, a teacher asked children to observe the weather on their playground. He suggested that the children paint or use another art material to show what they had observed about the changes in the weather. This art experience helped the children represent symbolically what they had seen.

Words become more meaningful when children are able to use them in context. The more related, in-depth experiences children are given, the more meaningful words become to them. For example, if children watch the same leaf on a tree change over a period of time, their understanding of the word *change* becomes more meaningful. Meanings for children are constructed in context, and this can be assisted through many planned experiences. When teachers talk with children about their ideas and encourage them to talk with each other, children are better able to construct and reconstruct concepts. Children's thinking becomes more explicit because they are using verbal symbols as well as thoughts. Likewise, children's thinking becomes more explicit as they express their ideas through artistic symbols.

The Zone of Proximal Development and the Concept of Dynamic Assessment

Vygotsky conceptualized the relationship between learning and development as the "zone of proximal development" (ZPD). The boundaries of the ZPD are formed by the lower level—the independent level—and the upper level—the maximum level. The independent level is what children can do without assistance, and the maximum level is what they can do with the assistance of teachers, other adults, and their more competent peers. There are various levels of assistance given to children within the ZPD. The ZPD is not static, but dynamic: It is always changing as the needs and accomplishments of children change.

Through the use of Vygotsky's concept of "dynamic assessment," both the lower and upper limits of the ZPD can be found. In order to determine the independent levels of the ZPD, the teacher must assess children to find out what they can do without assistance. Teachers can observe what children do, analyze their work, and keep records of their behavior. To determine the maximum levels of the ZPD, teachers may ask questions, make comments, and give cues or hints to identify what children can do with assistance.

To help them reach their maximum levels, teachers can encourage children to tackle tasks that challenge them and that are slightly beyond their skill levels. Teachers can structure their experiences with children and note how children use their assistance as well as what hints and cues are most helpful. Keeping anecdotal records, art portfolios, and checklists are all useful means of analyzing children's progress within the ZPD. When a child reaches the maximal level of the ZPD, the teacher plans what he or she will do to help the child move forward. The upper level of the ZPD now becomes the lower level, and the whole process begins again.

It is important to remember the teacher's role in children's learning, as supported by NAEYC:

> Teachers also take active roles in promoting children's thinking and the acquisition of concepts and skills. These roles range from asking a well-timed question that provokes further reflection or investigation to showing children how to use a new tool or procedure. (Bredenkamp & Copple, 1997, p. 115)

Vygotsky expands the idea of "developmentally appropriate" by thinking of what he calls the "future child" or what a child can do with assistance. Therefore, the teacher's instruction is aimed at the higher level of the child's ZPD. Whenever a teacher exceeds the maximum level of a child's ZPD, the child will usually walk away, ignore the work, refuse to do the task as asked, or act frustrated. This indicates that the teacher's activity is not developmentally appropriate for the child (Bodrova & Leong, 1996).

Using the ZPD in Visual Art

Teachers can use the ZPD to help children in any area of learning, including the area of visual art. For example, there are three 4-year-old children who are in the scribbling stage of graphic development. Mrs. Elkins has learned through observation that Tad has excellent motor coordination, but shows little interest in representing his experiences artistically. Ja-Niqua has very poor coordination, holds her crayon vertically in her fist, and makes straight marks on her paper; however, she shows a great interest in exploring art media. She frequently opens the magic markers and makes marks with them, and also shows an interest in brushes and paints at the easel. Ariel has good coordination, but is generally immature and has difficulty focusing or concentrating on an activity long enough to complete the task. After assessing what they can do, Mrs. Elkins plans activities within the ZPD for each child. She knows that eventually every child will be able to name his or her own scribble. She also knows that she must assist these children very differently.

When Mrs. Elkins sees Tad engaged in an art activity, she takes a photograph of him. She puts the photograph on the bulletin board and engages Tad in a conversation about the art medium he is using in the photograph.

> *Mrs. Elkins:* Let's look at this photograph. Who is this?
> *Tad:* Me . . . Tad.
> *Mrs. Elkins:* What are you doing?
> *Tad:* I paint.
> *Mrs. Elkins:* What do you use to paint?

Mrs. Elkins invites him to work further in the same medium. "Yes, you used red paint and blue paint. You used tempera paints and brushes. Would you like to use the tempera paints again, to make another painting today?"

Mrs. Elkins introduces Ja-Niqua to play dough and works side by side with her, while discussing the progress she is making in the medium. She says, "Let's see what we can do with this play dough. I can poke and squeeze my play dough. Now I am rolling it into a ball. What else can we do with our play dough?" They talk about how the play dough changes according to how they move it with their hands and fingers.

A field trip is planned for Ariel and her classmates to observe colors and shapes in nature. When they return, Ariel talks with her teacher about the trip. Mrs. Elkins writes down what Ariel tells her she saw on the trip: "Red leaves and orange leaves. Yellow flowers too." Mrs. Elkins uses a piece of lined note paper and begins a list:

> Red leaves
> Orange leaves
> Yellow flowers

The teacher asks, "What else did we see? Were there any green leaves on the trees?" Ariel responds, "Yes." Mrs. Elkins adds to the list:

> Green leaves

She asks Ariel additional questions to draw out more information: "Where else did we see green? What color was the ground around the trees?" When Ariel answers, Mrs. Elkins writes down:

> Brown dirt

She asks, "Were there any other colors in the dirt you saw?"

Now Mrs. Elkins begins to assess her teaching techniques to determine how effective they have been with each child. She continues to assess the children's progress as she works with them and changes her techniques until the children have reached their maximum art levels within their ZPD.

Learning is a matter of nature and nurture, not nature versus nurture. Both are important in the learning process. The mere availability of materials and tools in early childhood classrooms will not alone enhance children's art expression. *Adult input* is as essential to young children's artistic explorations as is an environment that invites them to express themselves artistically.

Children with Special Needs

Educators who work with young children who have special needs discover that the differences these children present are often differences in degree more than differences in kind. As Henley (1992) writes, "Although normal children may possess greater technical skill and control, this often has little bearing upon whether they evoke strong and expressive images in their art" (p. 8). Creative imagination plays such a vital role in the arts that very often the children's biggest obstacle is the lack of opportunity for expression. (Examples showing how classroom teachers can use art in working with children with special needs are presented in Chapter 6.)

Vygotsky believed that children with special needs learn in the same manner as typically developing children, namely, through social interactions between peers and adults. Children with a primary disability that prevents them from interacting normally with others can develop secondary disabilities that interfere with the development of higher order thinking (Berk & Winsler, 1995). For example, children who are partially blind or hearing-impaired may have difficulty working with their peer groups because they do not see or hear what other children see and hear. Therefore, they may develop a secondary problem: social isolation.

In many respects, Vygotsky was a forerunner of inclusion. Through use of his concept of the ZPD, teachers and parents can look not only at the weaknesses of children with special needs, but also at their strengths; their abilities are as important to consider as their disabilities (Guay, 1999; Rodriguez, 1984). Dynamic assessment can be used to determine which techniques are successful with these children and which are unsuccessful (Berk & Winsler, 1995).

Most of Vygotsky's research was with children who exhibited behavior problems in the classroom—impulsive, highly energetic, distractive, and disruptive children. We know today that working with these children often begins with fairly directive methods to reduce this type of behavior, often labeled Attention Deficit Hyperactivity Disorder (ADHD) behavior. Some of these children are on medication to help control their behavior in stressful situations. Vygotsky felt that children with special needs learn best in an environment in which they have more freedom to move and explore than in highly structured environments. These children need to be a part of the social, cultural group. If they are removed from their peer group, they can not develop social and emotional skills necessary for higher order thinking (Bricker & Woods-Cripe, 1995). Vygotsky felt that through social interaction, peer groups facilitate language and concept development and, consequently, higher mental functioning.

Art educators and art therapists agree that teachers should use sensory and manipulative approaches in art as they work with children with special needs, just as they would with all children in a good early childhood program (Anderson, 1978). They work to develop each child's gross and fine motor skills, eye-hand coordination, sequencing, and visual and auditory memory. Since art process and technique often follow a sequence of actions, they reinforce these areas of child development. At the same time that art activities strengthen the psychomotor domain and encourage cognitive development (Fox & Diffily, 2000), they also promote socio-emotional growth. As Alkema (1971) writes,

> When a child is given the freedom to express his own ideas as they relate to his own thoughts and feelings, he learns to think independently. Mental development is fostered. He is encouraged to be an individual, to be original in terms of self-expression. (p. 1)

When considered from the perspective of developmental appropriateness, "each child is a unique person with an individual pattern of growth, as well as an individual personality, learning style, and family background" (D. Varnon, cited in Very Special Arts Education Office, 1994, p. 3).

BALANCING THE VISUAL ART DISCIPLINES WITH CONTEMPORARY CONCERNS

The current postmodern climate, in which pluralism, complexity, and sociological differences are valued, supports a multicultural, gender-balanced, and racial-equity approach to art education. The category of "Art" has broadened to include a multitude of art forms, such as quilt making, batik, even topiary art. Persons identified as great artists in the traditional curriculum are not the only artists studied; artists known in other spheres are also studied. Children learn about popular arts as well as fine arts; and the crafts of other countries are valued for their aesthetic and educative qualities. Moreover, it is just as important that children learn about and work with living artists in their community, as it is that they learn about the art techniques and the work of the masters like Matisse and Monet. Children are encouraged to construct individual knowledge and understanding about the arts through their art experiences.

In these postmodern times, experimentation and discovery—key aspects of early childhood education—are valued for their contributions to constructivist pedagogy and extended to art education. As Walling (2001) points out, "In the visual arts, exploration and experimentation—true creativity—are valid ends as well" (p. 630).

The postmodern climate also values narrative and dialogue as much as the formal concerns of the modern era, usually interpreted as the composition of elements and principles of design in art, which are usually taught by art specialists. Today, writing and drawing are often combined in works of art, making interdisciplinary connections an interest in the art world as well as in the early childhood classroom.

It would seem that the time is indeed ripe for collaboration between art educators and early childhood professionals and for studies that emphasize the social and language aspects of early childhood art. Thompson (1988) writes about the relationship between young children's talk about their own artwork and the use of language in a social context:

> To the extent that the child's commentary is directed toward another person, her conversation also discloses understanding of the social context in which young children's drawing actually occurs and finds support. . . . As Gardner notes, the child soon recognizes in her drawing an occasion for shared experience. (pp. 9–10)

Research about the verbal aspects of art education, which we call "art talk," has helped to lay the foundation for collaboration, with studies ranging from children's talk about their artwork (Dubin, 1946; Gardner, 1980) and teachers' talk directed at children in preparation for and about their artwork (Douglas & Schwartz, 1967), to child talk and teacher-child talk about works of art by well-known artists.

CREATIVE ART EXPRESSION: THE REGGIO EMILIA APPROACH

There is a growing interest today in integrating art in the early childhood classroom, partially as a result of the widespread interest in the Reggio Emilia approach to early childhood education. In the preschools of Reggio Emilia, a town in northern Italy, the children spend time each day expressing their ideas through art media. Activities stem from the interests and ideas of the children. They have an active part in the planning of the curriculum, and their personal input is shown in their creative art experiences. The result is that children express themselves artistically in a much more mature way than most children their age (Katz, 1990).

In the Reggio Emilia approach, the arts are integrated into the school program as problem-solving activities, rather than as discrete subjects or disciplines taught for their own sake (Wright, 1997). Children's art making is emphasized to reinforce concepts, and their art products are considered to represent aspects of their learning. Visual arts are seen as an additional "language," one in which the children's ideas and concepts are expressed in art media (Edwards, Gandini, & Forman, 1998).

Perhaps the most innovative activity to evolve from the Reggio Emilia approach is a unique form of documentation. American early childhood educators are familiar with documentation in the form of note taking, video-taping, language experience, written comments, and checklists. However, in the Reggio Emilia approach, documentation in the child's own words is accompanied by artworks or photographs. The documentation panels display the child's work with great care and attention to both the content and aesthetic aspects of the display (Katz & Chard, 1996). The documentation describes in the child's own words—and sometimes the teacher's as well—the images, ideas, and processes represented by the child's art work. The documentation may appear on trifolds, bulletin boards, or charts. The words of the children or teachers are in large print, so that children, teachers, parents, and visitors can easily read them. This form of documentation makes visible the child's learning, since it often shows the processes of the art experience from beginning to end (Cadwell, 1997; Helm, Beneke, & Steinheimer, 1998; Hendrick, 1997). (Further discussion of documentation is provided in Chapter 5.)

BACK TO THE FUTURE: JOHN DEWEY AND THE ARTS IN EDUCATION

It is interesting to note the parallels between the Reggio Emilia approach and Progressive Education, active learning from firsthand experience (Barden, 1993). The Progressive Education of John Dewey was an antecedent to the Reggio Emilia approach; and Dewey valued the interconnection of home, school, and community, with firsthand experience in learning. He was a champion of the arts in education for their ability to infuse spiritual meaning into the activities and processes of daily living. Although Progressive Education in America emphasized learning by doing, it fell short of Dewey's focus on cooperative learning as social activity and on art thoroughly integrated into the overall curriculum. Today, in most elementary schools, art educators teach art as a separate course during specified times, perhaps once a week. Art educators who are certified for K–12 may know little about young children, but are asked to include pre-school and kindergarten children in their teaching schedules. Thus art educators and early childhood teachers may not have a common language with which to communicate, or even any time in the school week to share background knowledge and ideas.

Moreover, erroneous assumptions about the function of art in the early childhood classroom continue to exist; such assumptions include holiday art to "decorate" the school, scenery for plays, posters to advertise or advocate, or activities to "get a break" from real learning. This is a far cry from the specialized knowledge visual arts teachers have acquired in their study of the discipline: knowledge of media, processes, and art forms that represent past and present cultures, and knowledge of child art development. In this book we show how this dichotomy may be bridged through the application of Vygotsky's theories and a renewed attention to integrating visual art into the curriculum. The teachers and children we introduce in this book provide evidence of the great gains in—and enthusiasm for—learning when art is integrated into the early childhood curriculum. As John Dewey (1934/1980) emphasized in *Art as Experience*,

> Any idea that ignores the necessary role of intelligence in production of works of art is based upon identification of thinking with use of one special kind of material, verbal signs and words. To think effectively in terms of relations of qualities is as severe a demand upon thought as to think in terms of symbols, verbal and mathematical. Indeed, since words are easily manipulated in mechanical ways, the production of a work of genuine art probably demands more intelligence than does most of the so-called thinking that goes on among those who pride themselves on being "intellectuals." (p. 46)

2 Creating an Inviting Environment for Art Expression

In one classroom, different colored vases were placed on a windowsill. Deonta noticed the reflected light on the sill and floor. Looking perplexed, he said excitedly, "How did that happen?" He placed his hand on top of the reflections and said, "Look, now my hand is red, but I can't touch it."

There is no one way to arrange a classroom. Room arrangement will differ according to the ages and previous experiences of the children, the background knowledge of the teachers, and their willingness to experiment with new ideas. The goal is to create an environment for children that will nurture their explorations, language, and ideas. In planning their room environment, teachers should act on what they know about children and their development. Schirrmacher (1997) reminds us that "all planning is influenced by the values and beliefs one holds about children in education" (p. 249).

Two teachers were overheard discussing the arrangement of their rooms for the coming year:

> *Mrs. Brown:* I have a new classroom this year, and I want to think about what I can and can't change. You know I find it so helpful to use the natural light from the window as the children begin to explore with light, color, and shadow. I think I know where I want to place the table and easels, but I'm not sure.
>
> *Mrs. Jones:* I have taught in the same room for 3 years, and I would like someone to help me with my arrangement.

These teachers decided to work together to create an interesting environment for the children in their classes. Through collaboration, teachers can become more knowledgeable, competent, and confident in their decisions for planning room arrangements. By sharing ideas, teachers come to recognize that they often have the same problems. Through their discussions, they can find solutions to problems that may arise while arranging their rooms.

When teachers integrate subject matter, art can be explored extensively throughout the classrooms. For example, children can mix paints in the art area and find out more about color in the library area:

> *Jason:* I'm painting grass at the bottom of my picture.
> *Mrs. Anderson:* How did you make that mossy color of green?
> *Jason:* I mixed up the yellow and blue together and I painted my grass. Come over here to the library center. I want to show you this book about little blue and little yellow.
> *Mrs. Anderson:* What do you remember about this story?
> *Jason:* It's about yellow and blue mixing together.

When children can move freely among the learning areas of the room, the environment encourages them to carry ideas from one area to another. This allows the child a sense of completion of thought into expression.

AN AESTHETICALLY PLEASING AND FUNCTIONAL ENVIRONMENT

Teachers should ask themselves, "What are some of the things that will make my room more functional and appealing to children?" To help answer this question, one of the first things you, as a teacher, can do is to draw a sketch of your room. Then you can look at the sketch and determine if the furniture is placed so that it is aesthetically pleasing and functional. We recommend that the furniture for the art area include

> Water or sand table, or both
> Discovery table
> Art table
> Double easels
> Child-sized chairs
> Adequate storage shelves with clear containers for art materials

As you consider how to arrange the furniture and other objects in your room, we suggest that you keep the following points in mind:

1. Pathways between furniture give children more room to walk, make materials more accessible, and give classrooms a more open look.
2. Low shelves, open in front and back, are best for displaying objects at eye level.
3. Colored fabric, a variety of mirrors, and plants and flowers in attractive containers all make the room more pleasing.

4. Using a few artificial plants and flowers introduces children to the concept of both natural and man-made objects.
5. Culturally diverse reproductions of artwork displayed at eye level around the room can relate to the current theme and stimulate learning about artwork from different countries.

It is apparent to the children from the way the materials are displayed that they are there for them to handle and use.

Mirrors

In one classroom, differently shaped, nonbreakable mirrors were placed in each learning area. In the art area, a large square mirror was placed on the floor. The dramatic play area had a large round mirror bought at a local flea market. A stand-up mirror was placed on its side in front of the group area to encourage children to view themselves from different positions. Children lay on the floor so they could see "all of me." A full-length mirror stood in the writing center to allow the children to observe themselves writing.

> John said to Jada, "Let's take our paper and sit in front of the mirror to draw." The two children sat side-by-side in front of the mirror, drawing pictures of themselves. After they finished drawing, John said to Jada, "Look. I can see you. Can you see me?"

A few small mirrors were placed on countertops and shelves so that children could observe the reflections of nearby objects: a bird's nest, a shell, and a small wooden sculpture of a whale. In addition, a small mirror placed in the fish aquarium reflected the colorful fish. At a three-sided mirror, one child held a small pumpkin and said, "Look, there are three pumpkins."

Additions of Color

To add color to the plain brown shelves in the discovery area, a teacher added blue, red, and yellow pieces of art foam. Differently shaped red, blue, and yellow glass vases were placed on a windowsill. The children discovered the vases' reflections on the floor, wall, and ceiling (as Deonta described at the beginning of the chapter). The teacher suggested that the children place colored cellophane paper over the reflections on the floor. Excitedly, one child shouted, "Now the color is purple."

Reproductions of Paintings

Mrs. Anderson, a preschool teacher, introduced the artist Van Gogh by placing a large reproduction of his painting *Sunflowers* in the science area. In addition, she placed cloths printed with sunflowers in both the art and dramatic play areas. At first the children did not talk about the painting or the flowered print. Then one day Maria said, "Look," as she pointed to a sunflower on a visitor's blouse. Maria said nothing, but took the hand of the visitor, Mrs. Peabody, and pulled her toward the art area. Maria pointed to the reproduction of Van Gogh's painting and to the flowered cloth covering the science table (see Figure 2.1). Mrs. Peabody was surprised that Maria related the painting to the printed cloth and to the sunflower on her blouse. Mrs. Peabody encouraged Maria to verbalize what she saw by saying, "Tell me what you see." When Maria did not reply, Mrs. Peabody encouraged her to talk by describing the painting, the printed cloth, and the sunflowers on her blouse. Maria said, "They are pretty flowers."

Mrs. Peabody told the teacher, Mrs. Anderson, about her experiences with Maria. She learned that this was the first time any child had talked about the similarity between the picture and the flowered cloth. Then Mrs. Anderson talked with the children about the reproductions of Van Gogh's artwork and the flowered print. She realized from the children's conversations that they had noticed that the picture and cloth were similar, but had not commented about them. Sometimes children are aware of significance in what they see, but do not talk about it. A comment or question from a teacher will encourage them to express their observations. Later, when the students saw a reproduction of Faith Ringgold's painting *The Sunflowers Quilting Bee at Arles*, on display in the art room, Maria pointed to the small image of Van Gogh holding the vase of sunflowers and said, "That man looks like he is holding Van Gogh's sunflowers. We have a big picture of his sunflowers in our classroom." Later, Mrs. Anderson placed an arrangement of real sunflowers on the science table.

Living Things

When teachers decide to have plants in their classrooms, they should select some with colorful leaves. Plants with different-sized leaves, different shapes and sizes, and variations in color are interesting for children to observe and investigate. Animals will add interest to an environment, but their care is a matter of concern. When animals are included, the teacher must research carefully to see if the environment is suitable for the animals, and that no children are allergic to the animals. Children learn to relate to each other through the care of pets, although not all animals make suitable pets for the children. Keep in mind that if heat is turned off in the classroom over an extended holiday period, some animals may not survive, even when fed and given water.

Pieces of Fabric

Cloth can be used to represent seasonal changes. Children can bring in cloth remnants from home, or fabric can be purchased commercially. Texture, color, and patterns can stimulate children's language and concept development. For example, Mrs. Green's class studied polar bears during

FIGURE 2.1 Sunflowers are everywhere.

the winter season. She lay white furry cloth across a shelf in the room. As he entered the room, Remalio picked up the white cloth, wrapped himself in it, and announced, "I'm a polar bear. I'm all white and furry."

In the fall, one teacher draped material printed with apples and baskets across the shelf in the housekeeping area. She placed small baskets of red apples on a nearby table. The children did not comment about the similarities of the red apples to the apples printed on the cloth until they had eaten apples for a snack. Samantha said, "Look Mrs. Reed. These apples are red, just like those apples." Eating apples helped the children associate the apples on the printed cloth with the apples in the baskets.

Children's Contributions

Children can share in the active role the environment plays. For example, Mrs. Jones took her 4-year-olds outdoors to gather real leaves. They put some of them on clear contact paper that the teacher had stapled to the bulletin board with the sticky side facing out. They placed the remaining leaves on the art table. The children could manipulate the leaves on the table and classify them in various ways. The children admired the display of the leaves on the bulletin board. Jules commented, "Those leaves make our room look pretty."

Children should be encouraged to help make the classroom aesthetically pleasing. Mrs. Rice brought Indian corn, small gourds, and a large pumpkin into the classroom and asked the students to assist her with their arrangement on a table. After several children created an arrangement to their liking, they took tempera paints and created their own still-life paintings (see Figure 2.2). Later, the teacher talked with the children about the still-life paintings by Matisse and Cezanne that she had on display.

STATIONARY PROPERTIES OF THE ROOM

At the same time that teachers are thinking about beautifying their room, they should also think about the permanent properties of the room. On the floor plan of the room, note the answers to the following questions:

- Where is the source of water?
- Where is the water fountain? Is it a part of the sink arrangement?
- Where are the electrical outlets?
- Where are the windows, doors, and chalkboard?

Keep in mind that electrical outlets are needed for equipment such as language masters, listening centers, and overhead projectors. It is desirable to have the art area near a source of water for washing hands, mixing art media, and cleaning up. When rooms do not have a tiled area, a large sheet of linoleum may be placed on the floor in the art area. Having the art area near the window can provide natural light and extend children's experiences outside the classroom, as shown in the following example:

From a classroom window, a group of third-grade children saw the leaves of the maple trees beginning to turn yellow. Miss Turner asked, "What color are the leaves?" The children replied, "Green, and a little yellow." Miss Turner took photographs of one of the trees, and the children drew pictures of the tree in their science journals.

A month later the children looked at the same maple tree. Shakeesha said, "That tree's leaves are getting yellower." Miss Turner suggested that they find the photographs of the tree taken in September. After they looked at the photographs, Miss Turner asked, "Are there more yellow leaves on the tree than there were in September?" The children compared the tree to the September photographs of the tree. Then they drew the tree in their science journals and compared these drawings with the ones they had drawn previously.

During the winter they took their journals outside and compared their drawings with the real tree. They decided that

FIGURE 2.2 Kindergarten children's still life paintings are exhibited with their inspiration: an arrangement of pumpkins and Indian corn.

some trees have leaves that change color in the fall and that other trees lose their leaves in the fall. The children looked at their tree in the winter and spring and drew pictures of the trees and compared them to the original photographs and their drawings. In the spring Shakeesha remarked, "Oh look, our tree is beginning to have green leaves." Miss Turner encouraged the children to research trees on the Internet, discuss their findings about trees in group time, and write the important information they found in their science journals.

ARRANGEMENT OF LEARNING AREAS

The amount of space provided in a classroom for the art area is crucial. Open pathways help children move around the art area more readily. When space is limited, creative teachers will find new ways to store materials. A second-grade teacher who had little storage space placed plastic containers with materials under tables (see Figure 2.3). In a preschool classroom, there was adequate room for children to sit and draw pictures on trays under the science table. An alcove between two classrooms was used to place easels and drying racks. As the children worked at the easels, passersby stopped and talked with them about their creations. These conversations gave the children another opportunity to verbalize their experiences.

FIGURE 2.3 Materials are stored in plastic containers under a table.

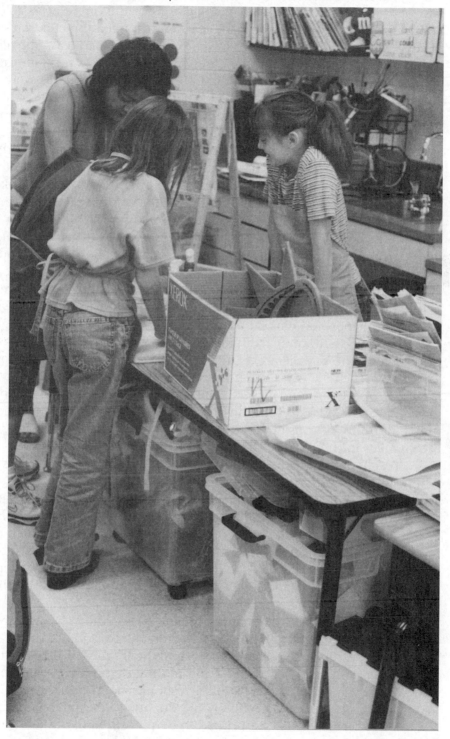

The arrangements of furniture and shelves can enhance or interfere with learning. Shelves can be used to divide areas and can be accessible from both sides. Mrs. Tuttle, a first-grade teacher, arranged the children's desks in clusters and encouraged them to share materials and ideas. She allowed the children to sit on the classroom area rug and provided trays for the children to use for writing and drawing. Comfortable area squares were available if children wanted to work alone. These children often worked in small groups or with one other child. Groups of children varied according to what was happening in the classroom and Mrs. Tuttle's intentions.

The art and science areas can complement each other since both need water and can use materials interchangeably. For example, the children in one classroom explored many magnets at the science table, then took them to the art area to make patterns and designs on a magnetic board. John said to a visitor, "Look, magnets can make pictures of things when I stick them to the board." Other areas also become readily integrated when their materials are used interchangeably. Picture books about artists and their works can be found in the library area. In the art area, Logan assembled various shapes of construction paper to make a collage as he looked at a book about Matisse. Designs also can be created in the math area with geometric shapes and pattern blocks.

In one classroom, magnifying glasses, color paddles, and prisms were on a table in the science area. One child, looking through a color paddle, said to her teacher, "Mr. Evans, you look red." Instead of replying, "Yes, I look red," Mr. Evans encouraged observation and problem solving by asking a question, "Why do you think I look red?" This question gave the child the opportunity to consider the relationship between the color paddle and the changes in the color of the objects that she saw.

Teachers may want to include a research area in their classrooms where children can investigate subjects that interest them (see Figure 2.4). This area should include books on art and other subjects. There can be a set of encyclopedias, *Childcraft* books, and magazines such as *Ranger Rick*, *ZooBooks*, and *Your Big Backyard*. Various clay and glass objects such as animals and pottery can be on display. (Children learn from teachers and other children to use breakable objects with care.) Art calendars and photographs from recent field trips can be included, as well as photographs the children and teachers have taken of other learning experiences. These are all examples of materials that the children can use to research any topic and increase their background knowledge for art expression.

Resources include the world of art and the world around us. Art books from the library, visits with artists, and natural objects all provide inspiration. Artists such as Matisse can help teach about shape and design; Van Gogh, about paint and texture; O'Keeffe, about color and value; and Bearden, about collage. For visuals, small art prints can be presented in baskets; and pictures from magazines can be contained in file folders or manila envelopes and organized by interest or category. Include pictures of sculpture and architecture along with paintings. All of these can help teach about the

FIGURE 2.4 A research center with books, art postcards, matching games and puzzles, patterning blocks, Cuisinaire rods, and tree branches gathered by children.

natural world and different interpretations of it in the arts. Local artists may be invited into the classroom to talk about their work.

Arranging the classroom by learning areas is not absolutely necessary for effective teaching. First-grade teacher Mrs. Ramos, for example, felt that when centers or learning areas were used, the curriculum was no longer integrated because each area and its materials were physically separated from the others. Her children knew where the materials were located and freely found and interacted with art materials when they felt they needed them to communicate their ideas visually. Therefore, art became an integral part of the day; it could relate to any topic of study. Mrs. Ramos, like many teachers of older children without a specific art area, keeps art media and tools in transparent storage boxes. She found that it was not enough to write a name on an opaque container to identify the contents. Seeing the materials in clear storage containers generated ideas. For example, her class was constructing a three-dimensional model of their hometown with small boxes, found objects, and art materials. One student noticed a small piece of blue cellophane and announced, "Hey everybody. I found a swimming pool for my house!"

Displaying Children's Artwork

Displaying children's artwork is an important part of the art experience and should be considered in the overall room environment. Katz and Chard (2000) state, "When tasks differ from child to child, achievement should be shared so that the new understanding can benefit the other members of the group" (p. 124). The ways in which teachers present children's work sends them a message about how their artwork is valued. Children's artwork can be placed in cardboard frames, picture frames, or on the backs of shelves covered with paper or cloth. When young children are hesitant to leave their artwork at school, color photocopies or photographs can be taken of their work and displayed in the classroom. The original artwork can then be taken home. Artwork should be placed at eye level, with each child's work represented.

In a second-grade class, children chose their own classwork to display on a hall portfolio (see Figure 2.5). There was space available for children to display one example each of their favorite work. They could choose their work from any subject area and change it whenever they chose. At the beginning of the year, these second graders seldom chose artwork to display. But by the end of October, they frequently chose their artwork. The teacher felt that their selections were influenced by the integration of art in the curriculum. She was pleased by the comments the children made to each other about their work. She heard remarks like these: "Look at my picture. I chose art, too"; "I like the colors you use"; and "I used several squares and triangles." The comments showed the teacher that the children had become involved in art talk.

Teachers can accompany children's artwork with documentation. The documentation may include photographs of the children engaged in various activities, accompanied by their written language or dictated sentences. A tape recorder can be used to record children's language for transcription. Multiple photocopies of the children's pictures and corresponding language can be made to use at school and to share at home. Documentation is particularly important as a means of communicating children's ideas to adults and other children. (Documentation is discussed further in Chapter 5.)

An Emotionally Safe Environment

The emotional growth of the child is as important as the cognitive growth. Children must feel secure in their surroundings to reach their full potential in their cognitive, physical, social, and emotional development. The atmosphere must be one in which a child thinks, "It is all right for me to make a mistake. It is all right for me to choose this color. It is all right for me to mix these colors together to find out what color I can make." It is essential that children are able to choose from a variety of materials, in order to learn what media work best to express their ideas.

> Shana said, "Mrs. Mitchum, look at all the colors I am using."
> Jay said, "I need some light red. Tell me how to make light red." Mrs. Mitchum did not answer him immediately, but asked if he saw other children who were making light red.
> Jay replied, "Oh, yes, I do. Mitchell is using white paint. I'll add white to my dark, reddish color and see if I get light red."

FIGURE 2.5 Children choose their favorite work to display. Often it is their artwork.

This child felt free to look at what other children were making, to ask other children's opinions, and to experiment with color until he had the desired color. Children are discouraged from using their imagination and creativity when teachers tell them what size paper to use and what colors to use, and when they are encouraged to make art products that are representative of particular objects. Mrs. Mitchum explained, "I want children to feel emotionally secure with their teacher, their classroom, and the other children."

Another teacher remarked that one way he reduced competitiveness was to accept all children's ideas. This teacher often responded, "Jack, that's a good idea. Tell me what made you think of that." Then the teacher would discuss the feasibility of the ideas. He emphasized effort instead of praise. Bodrova and Leong (1996) state, "For Vygotsky, the social context influences learning more than attitudes and beliefs; it has profound influence on how and what we think" (p. 9). The environment of the room assures children that it is all right to use their own thinking. Therefore, they can readily construct and reconstruct their own concepts.

CONCLUSION

This chapter highlights the ways teachers can create an appealing and stimulating environment for children. It includes a discussion of the importance of the attractiveness of the room and the arrangement of the room, and the significance of displaying the children's artwork and creating an emotionally safe environment. The classroom environment can serve as a powerful tool for teaching and learning, and the teacher should be receptive to changing the environment throughout the year as the children themselves change socially, emotionally, and cognitively. Note in the following example how one group of first-grade children rearranged their classroom following a visit to a farm.

> After they returned from the farm, the children moved several pieces of furniture in order to have enough room for their "sheep fold." Ms. Griffin agreed that they could move the housekeeping furniture out of the classroom to make an area for the sheep to graze. It was important that the children have enough space to play. Blocks were used to build a fence in the area for the sheep. The paper cutouts of sheep were mounted to other blocks so that they would stand up. Jane had a sheep with two legs. Marla said to her, "Why does your sheep have two legs?" Jane replied, "My sheep has four legs. You are looking at my sheep, and my sheep is looking at you. You can't see her back legs because they are behind her."

3 Art Media, Tools, and Technological Resources That Foster Language Expression in Art

"Teacher, teacher, can I use markers instead of these crayons?"
"Why is that, Chad?"
"Because I have a bright idea, and these crayons are too dull."

Teachers must be familiar with various art media in order to offer the children the media they need to express themselves artistically. There are many ways teachers can introduce art areas and materials to children.

MATERIALS AND TOOLS FOR ART EXPRESSION

Teachers at all grade levels are concerned about what kinds of art media to make available during the first weeks of school. When preparing for the new school year, as a teacher, you may ask yourself, "What kinds of art media should I put out, and how much is enough? What other kinds of materials do I need, and where can I get them?" In the beginning of the school year, materials should be familiar yet challenging. Materials should present increasing challenges as children progress through each grade level.

Art media can include an assortment of crayons, play dough, different sizes of slim and thick watercolor markers, colored pencils, pens, and paper in a variety of sizes and shapes. Avoid materials with scents, which may encourage young children to put them in their mouths. For younger and older children, tools should include a variety of paint brushes and scissors, as well as a variety of glues such as glue sticks, white glue, and craft tack glue. For older children, add a paper punch, stapler, and tape dispenser. A vast assortment of materials can be provided for making collages. Children's ideas can be represented through collage making long before they can be expressed graphically by representational drawing.

Artists take into account the physical properties and manipulative possibilities of the media they use in their artistic expression. In this regard, Forman (1994) has written about the different "affordances" of each medium. Because physical properties differ in different media, children need opportunities with a variety of art media to determine which medium would afford the best way to express their ideas.

Crayons

Crayons are familiar to most children and should be available throughout the year. Choose crayons that are soft and apply well to surfaces. Children will learn about crayons as they explore their properties; and through their accidental mixing of colors, they will discover secondary colors. Include fat crayons as well as the more common slimmer varieties. The removal of the paper from a few of the crayons will encourage the children to peel the papers off themselves. The tips, sides, and bottoms of the crayons will be explored and used as children discover what kinds of marks they are able to make using crayons. Crayon papers can be used for collage projects. When crayons break, encourage children to continue to use them. Stubs left from well-used crayons may be melted with an iron between waxed paper, or melted in cupcake tins over boiling water and molded into multicolored crayon chunks for further exploration.

> *John:* I'm going to make colors I've never made before with these.
> *Nathan:* Mrs. Whitehead, look at all the crayons I'm using. They are all together.

In a first-grade classroom, Mr. Petree placed flat, wide crayons of red, yellow, and blue in the art center. The children began to make discoveries about primary colors. JoAnne said, "When you rub real hard the yellow over the blue, you can make green." Mr. Petree used this opportunity to talk about secondary colors. The children sitting near JoAnne overheard the teacher-child dialogue, and said they wanted to try to make green. By making available the flat crayons in only the primary colors, this teacher set the stage for inquiry learning.

Occasionally, introducing a special type of crayon will spark a renewed interest in art making: glitter crayons, fluorescent, multicultural (i.e., crayons that represent various skin tones and highlights), metallic, and construction paper crayons. Children will find diverse ways to use crayons as they progress in their thinking and development.

Oil Pastels

A variation of the crayon is the oil pastel, sometimes referred to as Craypas, which is a brand name. Oil pastels require more initial teacher guidance, as they are oil-based and messier than crayons. After children have explored color mixing with crayons, they will enjoy the opportunity to use this different, but related, medium. Like crayons, oil pastels come in a variety of sizes, but they blend with more ease and will cover surfaces with more intensity than crayons. A white oil pastel produces a wider range of tints when blended with different colors. Newer formulations of oil pastels allow them to be thinned with water; pastels can be dipped in water and applied to paper, or a brush can be used to blend the colored surface for color mixing.

Paper

Paper is another art material that should be offered from the beginning of school. Be sure to offer different sizes, colors, and types of paper for the children to use (see Chapter 4 for how to introduce paper to children). When teachers have restricted budgets, there are creative ways to obtain the paper needed. Memos can be recycled for drawing. Newspapers, magazines, and wrapping paper can be recycled for collage making. Brown paper bags can be used for many kinds of art experiences, especially where strength of paper is required, as in mask making or the creation of stuffed shapes such as puppets or piñatas.

Paints

Paints can be purchased as powdered or liquid tempera, or in the form of tempera blocks, finger paints, or watercolors. Tempera blocks are much enjoyed for desk or table work. Although it is more expensive, liquid tempera is preferred to the powdered variety, as dry tempera paint can present a health hazard if mixed in the presence of children. Teachers should always look for the AP Certified Non-Toxic label on art materials they order. This label insures that the material is safe for use with children.

At first, teachers should limit tempera paints to the primary colors, so that children learn to mix their own secondary colors using brushes and containers. Later on, white and black tempera paints can be added for mixing tints and shades. Brushes are available in a variety of sizes, and chubby brush handles are easier for younger children to grasp. Anything that will make a mark is a tool for painting, such as combs, sticks, and plastic cutlery. Paper plates and yogurt lids can serve as palettes for mixing paint.

Children become excited as they discover how to mix their own secondary hues, tints, and shades (see Figure 3.1). Lem said to his teacher, "Look, I made brown." Ms. Stevens said, "Tell me how you made brown." When Lem replied, "I don't know," the teacher changed her strategy and said, "Show me how you made brown." She realized that the child was developmentally ready to show the process, but not yet capable of verbalizing it. Lem poured a little blue, yellow, and red in a lid and stirred with a brush. He said, "I made it with yellow, red, and blue paints."

Modeling Materials

Colored play dough and plasticine are readily available in grocery, drug, office supply, and variety stores, and can be ordered from early child-

FIGURE 3.1 These girls mix paints outside.

hood catalogs and art supply houses. Many teachers use recipes found in early childhood books to mix their own play dough, paste, and finger paint. Plasticine sticks should be broken into smaller pieces, so that they become more workable and pliable. Teachers should also offer wet ceramic clay throughout the year, as this medium contrasts with plasticine. It is wetter and softer, and can be air or kiln dried and painted. Access to a variety of art materials is essential for the artistic and cognitive growth of the child. All too often teachers limit the art materials to flat two-dimensional, but neater and cleaner, media. Yet children often make great strides in art development when they have the opportunity to explore their ideas in three, as well as two, dimensions (see Figure 3.2).

Natural Materials

Natural materials cost little or nothing and are easily obtained. Mr. Pete took the second-grade children on a field trip to see sheep being sheared. He gathered some of the wool and brought it back to the room.

FIGURE 3.2 A child manipulates clay to learn its properties.

The children washed, combed, and dried the wool and used it in their art creations. Susan said, "I am going to make a sheep with wool." She took some of the wool and glued it on the form of a sheep she had drawn. The same natural material may be used in more than one way. After the children had used the wool to design farm animals, Mr. Pete asked them, "Do you have any other ideas on how to use the wool?" Ibrahim said, "We can fill our baskets with wool and then it will be soft." Mr. Pete suggested that they experiment with dying the wool using onion skins, sunflower seeds, and dahlia leaves. He asked the children for other ideas of ways to color the wool. Responses included "ketchup," "Kool-Aid," and "beet juice."

Other possibilities for using natural materials may come from the outdoor school environment. Children often find natural materials on the playground, such as leaves, acorns, bird nests, sticks, and small rocks.

For weeks, Christina and Jamie picked kudzu leaves and pretended that they were umbrellas (see Figure 3.3). During the

FIGURE 3.3 Christina made an umbrella with kudzu leaves. Later, she painted a picture of herself with her umbrella.

fall, the children observed the colors of the leaves turning yellow. The teacher brought trays, paint, paper, scissors, and glue to use outdoors. Christina cut out big pieces of green construction paper to represent the leaves, and glued them onto the paper; then she drew herself holding the umbrella.

After a discussion of flowers in Ms. Bowen's kindergarten class, she placed a variety of cut flowers on the science table. The children brought flowers from their own gardens. One child discovered that rubbing flower petals on paper made colored marks. The children began "painting with flowers." Ms. Bowen continued to bring various brightly colored flower petals for the children to use. Several children suggested that they use the flowers to dye wool and other materials. Ms. Bowen encouraged the children's ideas in discovering how flowers can produce dyes. This is an example of integrating art and science by investigating to find out what happens.

ACQUIRING MATERIALS

Teachers must have a purpose for selecting the materials and tools for their classroom. How will the materials and tools they order help children in their art expression? Teachers can become familiar with the different types of materials and their uses by talking with other teachers, including art teachers, and by looking at exhibits at various conferences. Early childhood catalogs have sections where teachers can find descriptions of different kinds of art media and tools. Libraries in most schools have art catalogs that present materials that may not be included in the early childhood catalogs.

If possible, the teacher should experiment with materials before ordering them. Not only will teachers enjoy using the materials, but they also might discover other ways to use them. Mrs. Parker, for example, rubbed flat crayons across her paper to see the effects of her strokes. She found that they were much more difficult to use than the round crayons for color rubbings but better for color mixing. It is important for early childhood teachers to find time to sit with children and experiment with materials alongside them. A preschool teacher was observing a small group of students mixing paints and using them, when one child asked, "Mrs. Wright, would you like to paint too? I can show you how to mix colors. Guess how I made this pink color?" (See Figure 3.4.)

Another way in which teachers can find materials, particularly scrap or collage materials, is at yard sales and craft stores. A paint and wallpaper store might give teachers samples of paint color chips and out-of-date wallpaper sample books. Creative teachers can often find uses for materials other teachers have discarded. One teacher found Ansel Adams art posters from a discarded fifth-grade reading series. The black and white photographs interested the children, as they were accustomed to color photographs.

Juan: Could we make pictures like these?
Mr. Cheng: How would you do that?
Juan: Well, we have black and white paint.

When the children realized they needed gray as well, they began to experiment with mixing white paint with the black, much as they had done earlier when they used white paint to lighten other colors to make tints.

ORGANIZING AND PRESENTING ART MATERIALS

Art materials can be presented on low shelves—open on both sides, if possible—in attractive, inviting containers labeled with words, pictures, and real objects. If children feel safe in their environment and time is allowed to

FIGURE 3.4 These students are helping their teacher mix colors for her painting.

investigate, children will discover and explore the art media as well as other learning materials (see Figure 3.5).

Miss Smith, a teacher of young children, labeled her crayon container with a picture of crayons, the word *crayons*, and some real crayons hot-glued to the outside of the container. Pictures of art media are readily available in early childhood and art supply catalogs. One teacher used small clay flowerpots to hold sets of crayons and markers; she used puff paint and ceramic markers from a crafts store to label and decorate the clay pots. Another teacher presented small collage items like rice, beans, buttons, and beads in emptied tennis ball containers. The collage contents of these tall, slim, transparent jars suggest art-making purposes as they invite children to use their contents. Another teacher collected embossed jelly jars and pint-sized canning jars to present art materials.

Children must have easy access to materials, whether the materials are contained in plastic containers, clay pots, or other containers that may or may not be breakable. Some teachers have asked store owners to donate disposable display racks, which the teachers then used in their classrooms to display a variety of materials. Mr. Evans had a carousel, discarded from the library, in which he placed containers of crayons, oil pastels, colored pencils, felt tip markers, and brushes for children to use as needed. Children were encouraged to share materials with each other and to look at the materials that others were using. When children are sitting close together, they can share a variety of materials as well as engage in dialogue about the materials, processes, and their ideas.

FIGURE 3.5 Children construct with found materials.

Introducing the Art Area and Materials to Preschool and Kindergarten Children

Sometimes parents bring their children to visit their classroom and meet their teacher before the first day of school. Nicole and her mother stopped at Mrs. Grady's kindergarten room when Mrs. Grady was cleaning the aquarium.

Nicole: Look, there aren't any fish in the aquarium.
Mrs. Grady: Nicole, would you like for me to get some fish
   for the aquarium?
Nicole: Yes, I like pretty fish.

Later, Mrs. Grady put several colorful fish in the aquarium and placed it in the art area. Here the aquarium would serve as a focus of attention to encourage children to explore the art area. The aquarium provided children with familiar, aesthetically pleasing living things to enjoy. Mrs. Grady also set out several seashells, some sand, and a piece of driftwood. Picture books about fish were placed on the table, and displayed above the aquarium was a reproduction of Matisse's *Beasts of the Sea*, a cut paper collage of bold designs and abstract images cut from colorful pieces of paper. Mrs. Grady purposefully used the aquarium with living things as a tool to create interest, problem solving, art expression, and conversations among children and adults. Consequently, Mrs. Grady's use of the aquarium set the stage for inquiry learning. It served as a powerful tool for teaching as it drew children to the art area.

Teachers of young children find that introducing materials in the classroom should happen in a "natural" way. Young children are anxious to explore their environment. Knowing this, Mrs. Grady said to her new class of kindergartners, "Some of the materials in our classroom you already know about. Other materials may be new to you. Look around the room and tell us what you see."

After the children named and discussed things they recognized, Mrs. Grady said, "Let's walk around the room and talk about some of the areas." (In this activity a teaching assistant or parent volunteer can help with classroom management.) As the children looked around the room, several children suggested they revisit the "fish area." Mrs. Grady said, "Yes, let's look at the art area." Several children noticed the paper, crayons, sand, brushes, and paints. One child commented about the Matisse collage, "Look at the pretty colors in this picture."

As the children moved in and out of the art area, they began to play with the materials. The teacher observed the way the children used the art media and tools. One child chose a large sheet of red paper and made circles with a blue crayon.

> *Mrs. Grady:* Avery, I see you chose a red piece of paper and
>   drew some blue circles on it. Move your finger around
>   the lines you made. How does it feel, Avery?
> *Avery:* I go round and round like a circle.
> *Mrs. Grady:* That's the way your finger moves. How many
>   circles did you draw?

The teacher noticed that Avery counted the circles using one-to-one correspondence and assigned a number name to each circle. Mrs. Grady extended Avery's thinking by saying, "A circle is a shape. Can you draw any other shapes?"

The teacher's guidance technique is an example of teacher-child dialogue using art language. Sharp (1976) used the term *aesthetic extensions* to designate the way children's aesthetic concepts are extended or enriched through art dialogue in an art learning context. According to Vygotsky, social mediation happens between two or more people. This is called "interpersonal language" (Bodrova & Leong, 1996). Using interpersonal language, Mrs. Grady assisted the child's thinking by expanding his art experience. The integration of art and mathematics also occurred when Avery counted the circles and the shapes were identified.

Having the aquarium in the art area encouraged several children to draw fish. Victoria watched the fish for a minute and said quietly to herself, "I'm going to draw some fish." Mrs. Grady continued to observe as the children explored with the crayons. She interacted with a child who was marking his paper with several colors of crayons. Mrs. Grady said, "Find the orange line. Follow the orange line with your finger." Many teachers would respond to this mark making with statements such as "That's nice" or "Tell me what it is." These kinds of statements are patronizing to children and miss the opportunity for the development of art language and the construction of concepts that occur in a meaningful context.

Introducing Art Media to Primary Children

First grade and other primary teachers often have art areas in their rooms. However, primary teachers have more schedules to meet than preschool and kindergarten teachers. The following is the way one teacher introduced art media to primary children.

Mrs. Medlin, a first-grade teacher, said to her class at the beginning of the year, "Look around the room at the various boxes of materials. You may take the boxes off the shelves and explore the materials inside." Some of the boxes contained art materials, while others contained mathematical materials such as patterning blocks and wooden numerals. Other boxes were filled with science materials such as small magnets and magnifying glasses. Language arts materials included sandpaper letters, alphabet and word stamps, and finger puppets. The teacher explained, "The children readily integrate the materials through their work and play."

Mrs. Medlin asked the children to form small groups to explore the contents of the storage boxes. When the children returned to the circle, they reported what they had found in the boxes and where they were located. Occasionally Mrs. Medlin would ask, "How can you use this material?"

For several days the children continued to explore the contents of the boxes and discuss the materials among themselves. Mrs. Medlin continued to observe the children and noted what interested them. She saw that the children were particularly interested in the collage materials. She heard one child say, "This box looks messy." She asked, "Why do you think so?" When the child answered, "'Cause they're all mixed up," Mrs. Medlin asked, "What can we do about it?" Several children responded, "We can separate the stuff."

Mrs. Medlin offered additional containers, and the children sorted the materials using their own classification systems (see Figure 3.6). A few children classified by color, others by shape or texture, and a few classified by use. For example, things can be used to tie, like string, yarn, ribbons, and shoelaces. Through classification, art was integrated with mathematics.

Later, Mrs. Medlin said to the class, "Think about something you want to make with the collage materials. What kinds of material will you need? Use a tray to gather the materials you select. Bring the trays back to the group area." After the children had chosen their materials, Mrs. Medlin said,

> "Let's go around the circle and talk about what you selected.
> Ask the children around you about the materials they selected."

FIGURE 3.6 Mrs. Medlin uses containers to organize a variety of materials and manipulatives in her first grade classroom. The transparent containers are clearly marked.

Mary said to Emily, "My pipe cleaners are different colors and I can bend them. I have popsicle sticks. They are shorter than the pipe cleaners."

Pointing to Emily's materials, Jim said, "I know what they are. They are straws. Look what I found. I found pom-pom balls, paper shapes, milk jug lids, and I want to make a picture with round things. So I chose the stuff in this box."

The above conversations are examples of meaningful peer interactions. Vygotsky stresses that shared activities lead to development and learning and should not be limited to adult-child interactions only (Berk & Winsler, 1995). This kind of learning does not happen by chance. Mrs. Medlin is aware of the importance of teacher-child and child-child dialogue. She has planned for the children to communicate with each other by talking about their materials. She knows that shared experiences create opportunities for using verbal language and motivate children to become involved with art media.

Mrs. Medlin told her first graders, "You may work at your desks, on the floor, or at the counters near the sink."

Gloria asked her teacher for additional art media: "Do we have any glitter? I want to show my fish shiny and sparkly."

Instead of telling Gloria, "It's not out for this project. We'll use it later," Mrs. Medlin asked, "Do you remember where the glitter and glue are kept? You can take some to the table to finish your fish."

The child gathered some glitter in a cup and took it, along with a bottle of glue, to her desk. The other children continued to discuss their materials and plans with each other and the teacher. Mrs. Medlin encouraged the children to express themselves by asking specific questions about their materials.

> *Mrs. Medlin:* There are lots of ways to use pipe cleaners. Can you think of one way to use them in your artwork?
> *Mary:* The trees I saw yesterday were tall. I want to use my pipe cleaners for the tall trees.
> *Mrs. Medlin:* Jim, you selected some straws. How will you use them?
> *Jim:* I need scissors to cut them into little pieces for the limbs on my trees.

Some children did not have plans for graphic representations. They reported that they would paste all the materials they selected on their papers.

There are teachers who limit materials and put out only those that they believe should be used for the art project they have in mind. By contrast, Mrs. Medlin has given children ownership of their learning. She has allowed them to explore materials, choose what they will use, and share their ideas and plans for art making. The children have played an active role in decision making and problem solving.

USING TECHNOLOGY

Technology has many uses in schools today. Technology can be used as a tool to help communicate children's art to parents, teachers, school personnel, principals, and other children. In addition, technology can be a catalyst for children to meaningfully connect reading, speaking, writing, and other subject matter areas. It can motivate children to explore and continue to investigate art. It can help children revisit and reflect on firsthand experiences and examine what has happened in order to make new discoveries and decisions.

Overhead Projector

The overhead projector has been used in many creative ways by teachers and children. Children can place color paddles, colored tissue paper or cellophane, and mixed food coloring with plastic forms on the overhead projector to find out what happens to light and color. They can cut shapes out of paper and place them on the overhead to stimulate discussions of geometric and free-form ideas. Children enjoy exploring objects, such as pumpkins, whose shape is distorted by the light of the overhead projector. Vis-à-Vis pens can be used on overhead transparencies to explore line, shape, and color. Children can name the lines they draw, such as straight, curvy, zigzag, and talk about how the lines cross over each other. Children can draw pictures and tell continuous stories on the overhead. One teacher keeps a Ziploc bag with damp towels so that children can erase and change the pictures as they change the text of the stories.

Cameras

Polaroid cameras allow teachers to record and immediately document children's art activities and help children recall particular art processes. Documenting a child's involvement with art media will stimulate the child to continue to investigate art media. This is especially helpful with children who may hesitate to become involved in art activities. In addition, a set of photographic images can serve as a rebus of art processes to help inexperienced children recall the steps of art processes, such as how to mix paints and clean brushes or how to create a pinch pot in clay.

Teachers find that photocopiers are very useful for documentation. Enlargements of photographs of children engaged in art activities add dimension to documentation panels of children's artwork along with printed scripts of their dialogue. (See Chapter 5 for a discussion of documentation.)

Digital Cameras and Other Computer Technology

Photographs can also be enlarged by scanning and digitizing the pictures. A digital camera allows photographs to be printed immediately, without chemical processing. Computers, printers, and scanners streamline this process, and allow for flexibility with image size and type font. In addition, scanning artwork provides a record so that original artwork can be taken home.

After Ms. Walker talked about reproductions of still-life paintings by Renoir and Matisse, she gave the kindergarten children an opportunity to paint a still life. She placed a small box covered with cloth on a table. She arranged a variety of fruits and vegetables on top of the box: a large pumpkin (the focal point), apples, Indian corn, pears, and carrots.

In small groups, the children and teacher discussed how the arrangement looked from different points of view: front, back, and sides. The children and teacher discussed the colors, shapes, values, and lines found in the arrangement. The teacher used the same pumpkins, apples, carrots, and corn that the children had previously explored using their different senses.

The children used paint to construct a picture of the still life from their own perspective. Photographs were taken with the digital camera of the still life arrangement and the pictures the children had painted. These digitized photographs were enlarged on the computer to use on a trifold display board to document the art project (see Chapter 5). Teachers who do not have access to a digital camera can have regular color photographs enlarged on a color copier for use in their display panels.

Mrs. Raven, a second-grade teacher, developed a Power Point presentation to show children more story quilts created by the artist Faith Ringgold (see Chapter 6). For a third-grade science unit on weather, Ms. Patel used the Internet to find paintings of various weather scenes by artists whose work is represented in museums with Web sites. She downloaded a number of reproductions and integrated them into a Power Point slide show, which was shown on the classroom television monitor while the children created paintings about lightning.

Some teachers use computers for word processing as children write and illustrate books. Mr. Broderick, a second-grade teacher, asked the children to bring a three-ring notebook to school. Whenever the children learned poems, finger plays, or songs, Mr. Broderick typed them on the computer and gave the children copies for their notebooks and their parents. Using art media, the children illustrated the text of each selection on the page following it. Then the children took the literacy notebooks home in their book bags to share with their parents.

One child responded artistically to the nursery rhyme *The Three Little Kittens* by drawing and cutting out kittens and gluing them on construction paper. Then she cut out paper mittens and glued these on the kittens. Her illustrations were placed in the class literacy notebook for all of the children to enjoy in the library center (see Figure 3.7). The teacher also recorded the poems, songs, and finger plays for the children to hear in the listening center.

Videotapes

Videotapes of children's activities can show not only how children are engaged in art, but also how art can be integrated in all learning activities. For example, Mr. Cooper, a kindergarten teacher, frequently took the video camera outside. When the children saw caterpillars crawling on the trunk of a tree, Mr. Cooper videotaped the children watching them and talking about them. Some of the children gently touched the caterpillars and picked up sticks for them to crawl on. Back in the classroom, the children found pictures and information about the caterpillars in science books. Later, the videotape was shown to the children. The tape motivated the children to use art materials to make pictures of the caterpillars they had seen. Mr. Cooper also videotaped the children engaged in these art activities. When the videotapes were shown, the children often noticed themselves and made comments such as these: "I like my paintings better." "I can put a cloud in my picture." "Look at my pattern." "Can you make a tint like I did?"

One teacher asked the parents of children in her class to sign permission slips so that the videotapes taken of the class could be shown at parent meetings, teacher meetings, district meetings, conferences, open houses, and in class.

FIGURE 3.7 The children make a class book of their work.

CONCLUSION

This chapter focuses on the kinds of art media and tools that teachers can provide to encourage children's art expression and aesthetic awareness. We also talk about how to present materials to the children and how to use technology. Examples of art language are given for teachers to use from the beginning of the child's school experience. Examples also demonstrate how readily art can be integrated into other subject areas.

The use of worksheets and other handouts kill creativity in cognitive thinking because they show a prescribed recipe that results in a product that is not art. Art involves creative exploration, choice, and the child's own thinking.

> An art educator, walking down an early childhood corridor in an elementary school, saw examples of products that adults often refer to as "child art." On one wall she saw a row of paper-plate bears, followed by a row of mimeographed images that children must color in some classes. On the other wall, she saw 4- and 5-year-olds' artwork, beautifully and powerfully expressed, about farms and farm life. These works of art were on papers of different sizes and shapes. A variety of media were used, including markers, watercolors, and collage materials of all sorts. The works were wonderfully creative and often ingenious representations of the children's ideas and recollections of their experienced learning. The art educator knew, without entering the classroom, that the teacher of these children understood and valued art.

4 Beginning Investigations in Art

> A child stopped and looked at the classroom bulletin board to
> find his cutout bunny. He looked at each bunny carefully.
> Unable to find his paper bunny, he asked the teacher, "Which
> one is mine?" The teacher looked at the row of bunnies and
> could not recognize the child's paper bunny. Then she looked
> at the names on the back of the look-alike bunnies and handed
> the child his bunny. He said, "Is this one mine?" The teacher
> replied, "Yes, it has your name on it."

This activity illustrates a prescribed approach to cut-and-paste products.
The teacher selected the activity for the children to do. They had no choice
of materials, sizes, colors, textures, and, more important, no opportunity
to do their own thinking. The thinking was done for them. Children were
not given art media to explore, the choice of collage materials, or the time
to construct their own bunnies.

Jalongo and Stamp (1997) present the following four questions for
the teacher to consider in order to avoid the common practice of using "cute"
art and to promote challenging art.

1. Are the children's responses predetermined? If so, it is not art. . . .
2. Will one child's work look nearly identical to others? If so, it is
   not art. . . .
3. Who is the activity for? Is it simply to produce a product to please
   parents? . . . [then] it is not art. . . .
4. Will the child's effort lead to the creation of a new form that is
   satisfying to the child at his or her level of development? (p. 13)

An additional question teachers might consider is: "Why am I presenting
this activity?"

GETTING STARTED AT THE DISCOVERY TABLE

Piaget and Vygotsky stress the manipulation of objects and firsthand
experiences if children are to construct their own concepts (Berk & Winsler,
1995). A "discovery table" can help children learn about materials in depth.

The purpose of the discovery table is to give children the opportunity to play with different kinds of art media. By exploring with and investigating art media, children learn about creative and purposeful ways to use materials. They learn visual and physical properties of the media as they investigate possible means for art expression.

Each type of art media that children explore will evoke different responses from them depending on their background of experiences. For example, we tend to view paper in a limited way, to write or draw on. Consider how different from one another these papers are: drawing paper, construction paper, newsprint, foil, tissue, gift wrap, craft paper, typing paper, and cellophane. Some or all of these may be included on a discovery table (see Figure 4.1); each one will evoke different responses and ideas from children as they explore and investigate.

A preschool teacher, Mrs. Bryson, put out foil paper, drawing paper, cellophane, and tissue paper on the discovery table. The drawing paper was familiar to the children, while the other kinds were not as familiar. Mrs. Bryson sat with a small group of children and closely observed how they approached the paper.

> She asked, "What kind of material do you see on the table today?"
>
> Sydney responded, "Different colors of paper, and I see paper that I used at my day care center."
>
> Mrs. Bryson said, "Yes, there are different colors of paper. What can you find out about the paper?" A few children picked up the paper, looked at it, put it back on the table, and walked away.
>
> Joey announced, "I want to play with the blocks."

The teacher realized that the children were not interested in the paper and that she would need to plan strategies to help create interest in the paper exploration.

In planning for the next day, Mrs. Bryson decided to give the children more assistance, use more explicit language, and model behavior by introducing new concepts with actions. The next day she sat at the table and picked up a piece of aluminum foil and twisted it. As a result, the children twisted other kinds of paper. Then Mrs. Bryson looked through a piece of cellophane paper and said, "Oh, I can see through the paper. It is transparent. I wonder if there are other pieces of paper that I can see through." Immediately, the children began to pick up the paper and play with it. Joey, who was not interested in the paper the previous day, moved from the block area to join the group. Mrs. Bryson folded another piece of paper and the children followed her example.

> "I can't see through this paper," Joey said.

FIGURE 4.1 A variety of paper is on the discovery table, including construction paper and wallpaper, colored tissue and cellophane.

Mrs. Bryson responded, "If you can't see through the paper, Joey, try to find something else to do with the paper." Joey tore the paper and said, "I tore this paper."

During this exploratory experience, other children began tearing and folding paper. One child crumpled the paper.

Mrs. Bryson: Michael, what did you do to the paper?
Michael: I squashed it.
Mrs. Bryson: Yes, you squashed it.

Later the teacher used the word *crumpled* instead of *squashed*. However, in this experience, Mrs. Bryson accepted the child's language to describe his actions. This is extremely important. Children need support for their ideas if they are to continue exploration and verbalization. Children often imitate the teacher's behavior, and this motivates them to find new ways to explore materials. This teacher has had a direct influence on the children's learning. The intent is not for the children to copy the teacher's behavior, but to find other ways to manipulate their materials to discover new properties.

OBSERVING AND REFLECTING

As Mrs. Bryson observed the children, she made mental notes of how each child approached, handled, and talked with her and the other children about the paper. Later she transferred her notes to her plan book. These observations were the springboard for the next day's plans. Mrs. Bryson took in-depth notes throughout the year in order to remain current about the children's developmental level (for further information on how to observe and record children's behavior, see Cohen, Stern, & Balaban, 1997). Some of the important characteristics that she observed early in the year were hand preference, speech, enunciation, interest and exploration, language development, and attention span.

Teachers can also listen for children's knowledge of art language, for example, the names of primary and secondary colors and processes such as tear, paint, color, draw, and cut. Teachers can begin to use art vocabulary (see Appendix B) so that the words became more meaningful to the children. Unless teachers use art talk in context, the children will not be able to use these words correctly as they work with art media. Vygotsky emphasized that teachers have a direct impact on the way children think and verbalize their understandings (Dixon-Krauss, 1996). Teachers can use the Art Talk Checklist in Appendix B to record how the children's art language develops along with their art experiences.

Some children will begin to use the paper on the discovery table to make products with scissors, crayons, paste, and tape (see Figure 4.2). When this occurs, children can move from the discovery table to the art table to work.

In Mrs. Bryson's class the children began to cut construction paper into strips.

> The teacher asked, "Can you think of another way to place the strips so that they are not all laying flat?"
> Carl made loops and called them bridges.
> Ray told the other children his plans as he worked. He said, "I'm going to cut this piece of paper into strips." He used strips to make a boat.
> A few children linked the loops and said it was a slinky.
> "I called it that," Patrick said. "That's what I called it anyway."

During this shared experience, Mrs. Bryson encouraged the children to observe and to listen to what was said about the materials. She observed their ability to share experiences about their discoveries.

If teachers want to promote cooperation among children, they must listen to what children say and observe what they do. In the above example at the discovery table, a few of the children cut the paper into strips, made loops, pasted the loops together, and called the product a "slinky." If Mrs. Bryson had not been observing and had not overheard the children's comments, she would not have learned about the children's interest in working together and their ability to agree on a name for their product. To stimulate further problem solving and child-child interaction, Mrs. Bryson asked the children, "What other ways could you use the paper chains?"

FIGURE 4.2 One child cut and taped colored paper to construct a farm animal. Her teacher displays it near these farm manipulatives.

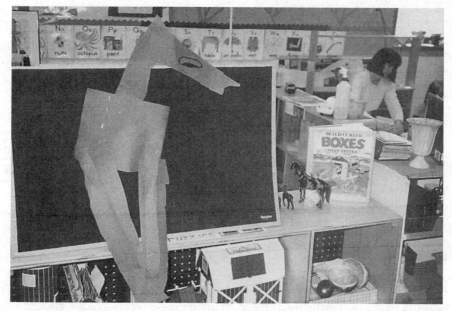

Some of the uses given for a chain were a dog leash, a dangling earring, a decoration for the room, a necklace or bracelet, an ankle bracelet, and, after adding more circles, a jump rope. To encourage further exploration, Mrs. Bryson asked, "Can you think of another way to use the strips?" Jimmy said, "Let's make a microphone." He twisted and looped the paper into an oval and said, "Now it's a microphone." Then he began to sing into the microphone. Two other children shared their paper strips and pasted them, seriating them from shortest to longest.

We suggest that teachers in the primary grades place a wider variety of papers on the discovery table. Older children show more interest in experimenting with paper than younger children. This may be because they have had more experiences with paper. The teacher's role is to work side by side with the children and to promote an awareness of the properties of the material. Mr. Marshall, a second-grade teacher, listened to the comments of his students as they experimented with the variety of paper on the discovery table.

> Carl said, "This looks something like gold. It is shiny, silver, and smooth."
>
> Clover took sandpaper and placed it under the construction paper and began to rub with a crayon. "This paper is bumpy," she said. "It looks like the mountains." Clover used the same process with tissue, wrapping, and foil paper.
>
> Jonathan said, "I cut the smooth, black paper. This one is rough. It will tear your skin off."

> Kristen tried to cut the sandpaper and said, "It is easier to tear."
>
> Taylor placed purple cellophane on a white piece of paper and said, "Now it is purple paint."
>
> James looked for smooth pieces of paper and compared smooth and crunchy (rough) paper. He put them in different piles.

Mr. Marshall noted that James had classified the papers by texture. He asked, "How are the papers in the pile alike? Are the papers in the second pile alike?" The teacher asked both divergent and convergent questions: What shape is the paper? (convergent) How can you use it to make other shapes? (divergent). Asking divergent questions gives children the opportunity to use their imaginations.

GUIDING CHILDREN TO EXPLORE AND CREATE

Children will use ideas in creative ways when they are in environments that are nurturing and when all ideas are respected. One of Vygotsky's tenets was that children learn through social interaction (Bodrova & Leong, 1996). In the example of the paper strips, Mrs. Bryson encouraged the children to interact with each other and solve problems. The children listened to each other's ideas and refined their already-existing concepts.

Wet clay or ceramic clay is another medium to use for exploration at the discovery table. Teachers can introduce clay by placing it in a container on the discovery table covered with a canvas cloth. Children should be allowed to decide how much clay to take from the container. The clay should be kept moist in plastic wrap before putting it on the table. The teacher may need to moisten the clay intermittently to prevent it from drying, but spray bottles should be kept away from children because they tend to overuse the water.

> In her preschool classroom, Ms. Martin asked, "What can you do with the clay?"
>
> Jim said, "I pounded it."
>
> Pat said, "I rolled it up; then I made a snake. I rolled it up because the snake is asleep."
>
> Ms. Martin asked, "How did you make it look asleep?"
>
> Pat replied, "I made it flat; then I rolled it up."
>
> Ms. Martin continued, "How did you make it flat?"
>
> "I hit it with my hand," Pat said, "like this."

Several children followed Pat's lead and pounded the clay until it was flat. Then Ms. Martin asked questions to focus attention on the texture of the clay. She asked, "How does your clay feel?" Some of the answers were "soft," "cold," "squashy," and "gooey." Jamaica said, "I can twist it, but when I do it breaks." Ms. Martin joined the children and began to manipulate the clay. "I am making a ball," she said. "What would happen if I pounded the ball?" "It would go flat," the children answered.

Ms. Martin continued to use art language with the children and encouraged them to talk about the texture of the clay and what they could do with it (see Figure 4.3). The children broke their clay into little pieces.

"What happened when you broke the clay?" Ms. Martin asked.
The children responded, "Now we have more clay."
Yoko talked to Lindsay about her little and big pieces of clay. The teacher asked, "Do they feel the same?"
They responded, "Yes, but some are big and some are little." "I'm going to put my little pieces together," Yoko said, "and I can make a sun." She put her pieces together and made a ball. "Look," she said, "it's the sun." Yoko compared sizes and said that her sun was bigger than the teacher's ball.
The teacher asked, "What other shapes can you make?"
"I can make a square," Jenny replied.
Ms. Martin said, "Outline your square with your finger." Then she asked," How did you make it?"
"I flattened it," Jenny replied.
Yoko said, "I can make a shape. I can make a circle."
She rolled the clay and twisted it into a circle.

It is important for teachers to use art talk and allow children to explore the media with their hands prior to introducing tools (see Figure 4.4). Tools for the children to work with may be introduced later, but in the beginning, tools tend to hinder the manipulation of the art medium, such as paper or clay, and therefore the knowledge of its properties. Throughout the year, many types of art media should be on the discovery table to extend the children's understanding of their properties.

Children need to explore in depth with the teacher's guidance. To know whether or not their guidance is effective, teachers must take notes and record the activities and guidance techniques that they used. When reading through their notes, they can decide whether or not the techniques used and the experiences given to the children made a difference in their artwork. The teachers can identify the lower level of the children's zone of proximal development through observation and continue to vary their teaching techniques until the top level of the ZPD is established, knowing that it will change periodically for each child. (The use of the ZPD is discussed further in Chapter 5.)

FIGURE 4.3 A teacher guides the children as they explore clay at the discovery table.

It is the teacher's responsibility to help children focus their attention, to think, to attend, and to remember. If children are to learn not only art, but to incorporate art into other areas of learning, teachers and children must work together to remember previous learning, as in the following example of a discussion of mixing paint.

> Mr. Bowers said to Joan, "Do you remember what colors you mixed together to make orange?"
>
> Joan replied, "No, I'm not sure that I remember. I think I used red."
>
> Mr. Bowers prompted, "I saw you using red and mixing it with another color. Can you remember what it was? Let's look at the colors that are here on the easel." Joan looked at the colors and still had a problem remembering. Then, Mr. Bowers suggested, "Try using yellow and let's see if yellow and red make orange."
>
> Joan mixed the two colors and said, "I remember now. It's yellow and red. If I mix them together, I can make orange."
>
> Mr. Bowers asked, "What other colors can you make with the paints that you have on the easel?"

Helping children to remember can be enhanced by taking photographs of children as they work together (see Chapter 5 for more discussion of documentation). Having photographs to look at provides continuity to children's learning and makes it easier for them to remember what art media and processes they were using and what discoveries they made (see Figure 4.5).

FIGURE 4.4 By discussing the likenesses and differences among art materials, this teacher encourages children to organize objects using classification.

MAKING CONNECTIONS ACROSS SUBJECTS

The materials found on the art discovery table, such as paper, clay, and natural objects, can be integrated into any subject that is being discussed in the classroom. These materials can become an integral part of what is happening in the classroom. For example, in the area of mathematics and science, most teachers talk about material objects. Children can sort the objects, talk about how they are alike and different, and classify them into groups that are alike in some way. Older children are capable of putting objects together according to their uses. This is a more sophisticated form of classification, but is necessary for the understanding of addition. Children can talk about how many objects are in a group, put them into one-to-one correspondence to make comparisons, and add additional objects to a group to make one set larger than the other.

Playing with objects helps children learn concepts such as alike and different, living and nonliving, and real and not real. These concepts are important in the teaching of science and social studies. For example, in Mrs. Goodwin's first grade, a group of children were talking about animals in their habitat. They were particularly interested in ocean animals, and the teacher encouraged them to do research on an animal of their choice. The children made a trip to the library to bring additional books to the classroom. They listened to music about the ocean, and they saw videotapes about different kinds of ocean animals. They were particularly interested in the whales and sharks. After they had done the research, Mrs. Goodwin asked the children to make a representation of the animal that they had chosen and to put the

FIGURE 4.5 Children learn about color and technique as they experience paint at the easel. The photograph their teacher took helps them remember what they learned.

animal in its habitat. They could use any art materials they chose, such as various types and sizes of paper, paints, and found materials (see Figure 4.6). The children decided to make an ocean mural. Some children drew ocean animals and plants, painted them, and cut them out. Several children painted the sea, including a horizon and sky. Other children arranged and pasted the painted cutout shapes, along with found objects and images from nature magazines, onto the painted ocean backdrop, completing the mural.

There are many interesting research findings that were evident in the children's art expressions. The art process actually helped the children learn more about the ocean animals as they worked to reconcile the properties of the different art media with their ideas for representation. It was necessary for the children to reflect on what they had discovered about the animals in their habitats. The children had to revisit what they had learned and decide what was important for them to include in their artwork. They communicated their ideas about animals to each other. Sometimes the children looked at each other's artwork and discussed it.

> *Janet:* I like the shark you're drawing.
> *Sam:* I'm going to make eyeballs on my shark.
> *Janet:* Do you know what kind you are going to make? Did you do your research?
> *Sam:* Yes, I did, and I am going to draw my picture so that there is an eyeball on only one side of the shark. I want to show that the shark is swimming on its side.

Plate 1 Four-year-old Megan and her classmates had studied plant growth. Megan told Mrs. Wright what she knew about flowers. She identified the cut paper shapes, and her teacher wrote Megan's words on a transparency which could be lifted to reveal the artwork underneath. The transparency allows Megan's artwork to be appreciated in two ways: as art, and as documentation of what Megan knows about plants.

Plate 2 Megan used larger and smaller circles to draw three flowers. She crayoned with realistic colors for the flower, leaves and stems, and the dirt in which they are planted. Then Megan added strips of green cellophane and silver metallic paper to represent grass and thereby created a "mixed media" artwork.

Plate 3   Megan broadened her understanding of media and skills in technique as she explored paint along with crayon. The crayon-traced circles resist the paint and help to differentiate the flower centers from the petals. Megan has discovered an "affordance" (Forman, 1994) about the way different art media work and express.

Plate 4   During the Fall, Megan and her classmates learn that trees lose their leaves. By asking Megan about her painting, Mrs. Wright learned how she understood this concept, and included their conversation in the display of student artwork in the corridor outside her classroom.

Megan: There are beautiful leaves falling.
Teacher: Where else did you paint leaves?
Megan: There are leaves in the grass.
Teacher: Why are the leaves in the grass?
Megan: They have already fallen from the trees.

Plate 5 Throughout the winter, Megan experimented with different painting processes. The description of her artwork includes information about Megan's art processes, imagery, ideas, and feelings.

Megan

I splattered the snow.
Then I made the deep snow.
Then I painted snowballs
The children ice skate on the pond. I love the pink.

Plate 6 When Mrs. Wright introduced her students to the artwork of Claude Monet, Megan became very interested in making lighter and darker colors. She mixed white with various color hues to make tints, and black with various color hues to make shades.

Megan looked at Monet's pictures of water. As she looked through calendar pictures of landscapes and waterfalls she decided to paint a waterfall. Megan expressed that she noticed different shades of green trees. Some were light green and others were dark green Megan discovered how to use white to create the lighter shades of green. She shared with the class that there are two

waterfalls in her picture. They are far away from each other.

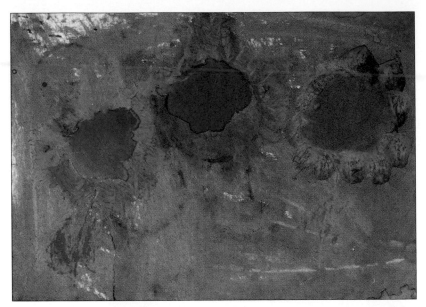

Plate 7 By spring, Megan had returned to painting flowers. She used complementary hues of red and green paint over crayon drawing, creating great visual impact in her painting.

Plate 8 As described in Chapter 5, Megan decided to make a painting like the reproduction she enjoyed of Renoir's *Bouquet of Chrysanthemums*. Mrs. Wright and Megan talked about her use of horizontal, vertical, diagonal, and curved lines in the painting. They also talked about the similarities and the differences in geometric circles and the organic shapes of the flowers and butterflies. Butterflies are not in Renoir's painting, but Megan has added them to her painting. The butterflies add additional interest to the painting.

FIGURE 4.6 Children select art materials to use with their ideas for their mural.

> *Mrs. Goodwin (overhearing the conversation):* What are you
>   going to use to make the eye?
> *Sam:* I'm going to use a button. I want to make waves.
> *Mrs. Goodwin:* How are you going to make waves?
> *Sam:* I'm going to use a toothbrush and move it back and
>   forth on my paint and see if that looks like waves.

Moving the toothbrush back and forth, Sam made a few lines on the blue
paint.

> *Sam:* Look, I think that looks like a wave.

The children around him agreed that he made "good waves." While the
children were working, Mrs. Goodwin went from child to child comment-
ing on their artwork.

> *Mrs. Goodwin:* I see that you covered your paper in blue,
>   Sara. Can you tell me more about it?
> *Sara:* Because my whale is under the water and all you can
>   see is the blue. See those little pink lines there.
> *Mrs. Goodwin:* Tell me about them.
> *Sara:* That shows where my whale is moving under the water.

Two children were working together to make a dolphin.

Trevor: I'm working with Jane to make a dolphin.
Mrs. Goodwin: Is your dolphin jumping out of the water?
Trevor: No, my dolphin is just swimming along.

When the children had finished, Mrs. Goodwin asked them to write a sentence about their artwork. Later they read their sentences to the class and told the class about how they had used various art media.

In these activities, Mrs. Goodwin had incorporated the language arts through listening, speaking, writing, and reading. She had included art expression to encourage the children to use their knowledge from their research. Talking with each other and their teacher about their paintings and collages gave the children the opportunity to share their knowledge and artwork. Art became an avenue to express what they knew about their animals.

Although perhaps not as obvious as science, mathematics was very much a part of what the children were learning. Spatial understanding was evidenced as Sam showed a shark swimming on its side by showing only one eye. Sara showed that you could look down on the ocean without seeing land, and locate animals by drawing waves in the water. Art may be integrated into all areas of learning, whether the curriculum is integrated, or whether it is oriented more toward separate subject matter areas.

CONCLUSION

The discovery table can be used to introduce various art media to children. The art media should be varied and carefully selected so that children can learn about the individual properties of each medium. Teachers who listen carefully to what children say, and watch closely what children are doing with the media, can ask purposeful questions and make appropriate comments about the children's use of the media.

Thinking teachers use their experience and knowledge to make decisions. They know their subject matter well and are willing to learn with children. They know how to use art language and how to encourage children's art expression. This does not happen by chance. These teachers keep careful notes to determine which strategies are most effective with individual children. They ask themselves, "Will these same techniques be effective with another group of children, or with one child, or perhaps in another activity?" They are alert to what is happening with the children as they express themselves artistically. What are they doing? What are they saying? What did they find out? Teachers think about, "When will I know that each child has arrived at a higher level of performance? Has she or he reached it, and now am I ready to go ahead and plan further for this child?"

One young painter expressed his knowledge about the art medium he was using and the subject matter he was painting in conversation with his classmates:

This is the ocean. Blue for the ocean. The top part is purple for the ground. I mixed all different colors together, because I learned in a book that you can mix all colors, lots of colors, together and make all different colors. I showed the blue ocean with my blue paint, and I used my purple paint to show the beach. That's the seashore.

5 Guiding Children's Art Through Language

> *Austin:* I want my tree to have leaves. Gee, I wonder how I can figure that out.
>
> *Myleah:* Well, I just think about it. Then I know.

Language is a mechanism for teachers to use in guiding children's cognitive development and ability to express their knowledge about their world. According to Vygotsky, language leads development and is the primary source of mental development (Berk & Winsler, 1995). Children's cognitive development and skills are transformed by their social surroundings when they interact with other, more capable, children and adults. If teachers want children to use art as a way to show what they know, they must provide them with in-depth experiences. In order to restructure present understandings and construct new concepts, children must explore ideas in a variety of situations.

ASKING CONVERGENT AND DIVERGENT QUESTIONS

Teachers can limit children's responses to one right answer by asking convergent questions. There is a place for convergent questions when one right answer is required. Divergent questions encourage thinking in many different directions and reveal how children think about a problem. For example, the convergent question, "What color did you use to paint this shape?" has only one answer. A divergent question such as "What ideas did you have when you painted these shapes?" encourages children to reflect on the processes they used to develop the artwork. Too often teachers ask convergent questions without realizing that they have limited the children's thinking processes.

During art experiences teachers should use the types of questions that will elicit thinking and discussion among children and teachers. In order to challenge children, teachers can ask many open-ended questions about art processes, such as the following:

How did you use these materials?
What did you find out about the shiny paper?
How were you able to repeat this line?

Children's answers to questions determine whether teachers need to re-phrase their questions or statements. For example, a first-grade teacher said to Maria, "I see a dog in your picture." Maria answered in a frustrated tone, "That's not a dog; that's my mama." Realizing his mistake, Mr. Allen responded, "Tell me more about your mother." This gave the child the opportunity to give more details about the picture.

To further encourage children to talk about their artwork, teachers may say, "Please tell me more about your picture." or "What would you like to say about your artwork?" Both examples are open-ended and elicit further discussion. Children's use of language should be accepted. For example, second grader Isabel said, "I have two kitten in my picture." Ms. Haines responded in a positive way, "Yes, I see two kittens in your picture." Instead of focusing on Isabel's grammar, the teacher had focused on the artwork. Some children speak with a distinct dialect, and teachers need to be knowledgeable about cultural differences in children's language.

ART TALK

Teachers should offer children models of art talk (Schirrmacher, 1997; Sharp, 1976). Appendix B provides classroom teachers with information about the language of art, which is familiar to art educators. In a school that has an art specialist, it is helpful for the children if both teachers collaborate to use terms such as *color, line, shape, texture,* and *space,* and refer to *balance, pattern, emphasis, movement, proportion, unity,* and *variety.* For example, a teacher might say, "I see one fat zigzag line and two thin straight lines," or "I get a happy feeling from the warm colors you used." They should ask children questions that stimulate further discussion about art (Hamblen, 1984; Taunton, 1983), such as

How did you get that light pink color?
Tell me about the shapes you used.
How does the texture of the clay feel to you?
Where did you get your idea?

When third grader Shirley showed her drawing of a butterfly to her teacher, Ms. Mack said, "Look, Shirley, your butterfly is the same on both sides. See, its wings are the same shapes, and you have put a wing on each side of its body. Your picture shows symmetry because this side looks the same as that side. Symmetry is one way artists balance their artwork."

Often children are overheard making comments and expressing their ideas to each other while they engage in art:

See my fast lines.
Look at the way I've made a pattern with my green and red dots.
First green, then red, then green, then red, all over my paper.

See how I've mixed my yellow and orange paint. I'm using happy
colors because I'm making a happy picture.

My idea is about the aquarium. I want to show big and little fish
swimming fast, 'cause the big fish is going to eat the little fish, so
I'm making fast lines behind my fish.

When teachers overhear children using art vocabulary in talking about their
own and other's artwork, they know that their modeling of art talk has
made an impact.

USING THE ZPD AND DYNAMIC ASSESSMENT

By observing children's use and interest in art media, teachers can
assess their knowledge of art. From an examination of the Art Talk Checklist found in Appendix B, Mrs. Parks, a kindergarten teacher, was able to
determine how familiar Cody was with art vocabulary. She found that Cody
could not name the primary colors—red, blue, and yellow. Mrs. Parks took
the children outdoors to play at their favorite spot, a large elm tree. While
the children were outdoors playing, Mrs. Parks invited Cody to help her
pick up fallen leaves.

Cody picked up a leaf and said, "It's like yours."
Mrs. Parks replied, "Yes, the color of your leaf is yellow,
just like the color of my leaf." Then Mrs. Parks asked, "Cody,
how many yellow leaves can you find that are the same color
as your yellow leaf?"

Her response helped Cody feel successful. Children's motivation for learning is tied closely to their successful experiences. Cody found more yellow
leaves, and then proudly arranged them on a tray.

This learning experience did not happen by chance. Mrs. Parks was
aware of Vygotsky's concept of the zone of proximal development—the
area that lies between the child's independent level and maximum level of
performance. In this case, Cody's independent or lower level was that he
could occasionally name the primary colors with assistance. However, Mrs.
Parks knew that if she wanted Cody to learn color names, she had to challenge him beyond his present, independent level. She wanted to guide Cody
effectively in order to reach his maximum, or upper level, which was to
name the primary colors consistently.

Now that Cody can name the color yellow, Mrs. Parks's instructional
techniques will change. Her plan at the moment is to encourage Cody to
bring in many different colored leaves from the playground. She will continue to encourage Cody to match the colored leaves and provide him with
assistance when needed. Through other experiences with leaves and art
media, Cody will learn to name the primary colors without assistance.

To guide children's learning effectively, it is important for teachers to follow the children's lead (see Figure 5.1). Mrs. Parks responded to what Cody knew: his leaf was the same color as his teacher's. One way Mrs. Parks assessed Cody's growth was through the concept of dynamic assessment. Dynamic assessment is an outgrowth of the ZPD. It is ongoing, authentic assessment which tells teachers whether or not their teaching strategies are effective. Through dynamic assessment, teachers can make plans to effectively continue working with children until they reach their maximum levels. Dynamic assessment is not complicated or difficult for teachers to use. It simply means identifying where children are at the present time and helping them move forward in their learning and development. For example, Mrs. Parks provided Cody with yellow crayons and tempera paints. Later, while painting at the easel, Cody said, "Look teacher. I painted yellow." While Cody was making a collage, Mrs. Parks asked him to pick out some yellow pieces of material. Cody did not hesitate to choose yellow. Through similar experiences, Cody learned the colors red and blue. When teachers identify a child's ZPD, it tells them what the child knows and is capable of learning. To find out what the child can learn, the teacher can give cues, hints, and other assistance. Teachers will know when they have gone beyond the children's maximum level of learning. When teachers push children beyond their level of understanding, they may lose desire to learn, become frustrated, or ignore the task.

DEVELOPING CURRICULUM BASED ON CHILDREN'S KNOWLEDGE AND INTERESTS

Paying careful attention to children's levels of independent and assisted performance can help teachers in their curriculum planning. A first-grade teacher, Mrs. Gamble, began the school year with the theme "Children in Our Classroom." This theme became the focus of interest for defining how the subject areas, including the arts, would interact to form an integrated curriculum. Mrs. Gamble wanted the children to become acquainted with, recognize, and respect their likenesses and differences, and interact positively with each other.

Mrs. Gamble was thinking about possible ways to introduce the theme when she overheard comments from the children playing at the sand table.

John: Look. My hands are under the sand.
Lisa: My hands are next to yours.
Manuel: I can hold sand in my hands.
Sarah (to Kia): My hands don't look like yours. Yours look black.
Vanessa (to Kia): My hands are black because I am Black. You are Black too.
James: My hands are brown. I'm Black too.

FIGURE 5.1 Children tell the teacher what they want to learn about color.

Kia and Vanessa (to the other children): You're not Black like us.
Lucy: Well, I'm White.
Kia: But you don't look White.

Mrs. Gamble decided that the children's interest in their skin color would be a good way to introduce cultural diversity and the theme "Children in Our Classroom." Kia's comment showed her that these children did not associate race with the color white, which they associated with white papers, crayons, paints, or chalk. Mrs. Gamble took Polaroid pictures of the children as they played in the sand. The pictures gave the children the opportunity to reflect on how they were using their hands to play with the sand. They matched individual colors from sets of multicultural crayons to the skin colors of their classmates. They mixed their own colors of paint to match their skin tones. Excitedly, they painted the bottoms of their hands and made hand prints on paper.

From listening to the conversation among the children, Mrs. Gamble knew that the topic she had chosen had high child interest and met the following criteria for choosing a topic of study:

- Real world application
- Meaningful context
- Readily available materials
- Age appropriate
- Flows from week to week/month to month (*Integrated Curricula Theme Criteria*, 1994)

The above criteria may be used by teachers to choose any theme, unit, or topic that they plan to integrate. Art can become an integral part of the learning and is a natural avenue for children to express and articulate their ideas. For example, drawing is considered prewriting for young children. It involves lines, shapes, and space. Children communicate what they are thinking by using a variety of art media (see Figure 5.2).

Complementary to the child-centered principles for curriculum integration listed above are the subject-oriented standards of the National Art Education Association. These are presented in Chapter 7 as an opportunity for rich collaboration between classroom teachers and art specialists.

USING THE IMMEDIATE ENVIRONMENT TO MOTIVATE ART EXPRESSION

In the spring, Mrs. Wright, a teacher of 4-year-old children, brought in fresh flowers from her garden and placed them in the science area. Mrs. Wright placed vases of different sizes and colors on a table. When the children began to bring flowers from home, they arranged them in the vases they selected. Some of the children placed their vases on the science table, while others placed them in different areas of the room.

> *James:* It looks like a spring garden.
> *Victoria:* I think my pink flowers look real pretty on the
>   windowsill.

Some of the children brought in artificial flowers. Mrs. Wright used this opportunity to discuss living and nonliving things. The children discovered that artificial flowers never wilted.

> *Megan:* These flowers are fake.
> *Mrs. Wright:* Tell me more about these flowers. Why do you
>   think they are fake?
> *Megan (picking up flower petals from the table):* These fell off
>   the purple flowers. Nothing fell off the red flowers.
> *Mrs. Wright:* Are you surprised? How could that happen?
> *Megan:* Because they're not real. These are real flowers. I
>   can smell them. I can't smell the fake flowers.

There were several art reproductions displayed in the room near the vases of flowers. Mrs. Wright pointed to the reproduction of a Renoir painting of flowers. She asked, "What would you say about these flowers?"

> *Megan:* I think that's just a picture of flowers.
> *Mrs. Wright:* Yes, you're right, Megan. An artist named
>   Auguste Renoir painted these flowers.

FIGURE 5.2 Taylor, age 6, watched the gerbils inside the gerbil ball and communicated what he saw by drawing a circle around the gerbil to show the ball.

Megan moved the Renoir print to the art area and began painting flowers. She had been mixing tempera paints during the year. To Mrs. Wright's surprise, Megan immediately started experimenting with different shades and tints. Mrs. Wright observed Megan attempting to match the colors in the Renoir print to her own color mixtures.

> Megan called to Mrs. Wright, "Look teacher, I'm making that picture." Mrs. Wright asked Megan to tell her more. Megan explained, "I'm copying Mr. Renoir's painting of flowers." She pointed to a flower and said, "This flower looks reddish purple."
>   Mrs. Wright asked Megan, "What colors of paint do you need to mix together to make a reddish purple color?" Megan responded, "I think I'll try some blue with red."

Megan continued to mix the colors. She painted tall flowers in her picture. She worked for several days on this painting, experimenting with colors until she was satisfied with her work of art. She would periodically call the teacher over to talk about her work.

> *Mrs. Wright:* How did you create the different shades of
>   green in your picture?
> *Megan:* I added some blue to that yellow and made it dark green.
> *Mrs. Wright:* What do you plan to make next?
> *Megan (pointing to the Renoir picture):* I want to paint more
>   pink flowers like those.

Megan's enthusiasm and tenacity for copying a work of art was unusual for a child so young. Her mother came to the classroom several times to admire Megan's work. The parental interest motivated Megan to continue painting the flowers until she was satisfied with her work.

One afternoon, Megan announced that she was finished with her work. Mrs. Wright looked at her painting and asked, "Do you want to add anything else to your painting?" Megan looked at the Renoir reproduction and said, "Oh, I forgot to paint the vase." She immediately began mixing paints. Mrs. Wright had a purpose for the way she worded her question. Instead of telling Megan that she forgot to include the vase in her painting, she allowed Megan to reflect on her artwork and make her own decisions.

When the principal visited the room, he was so pleased with Megan's picture that he asked the teacher if she would put it in the display cabinet in the hall. When Mrs. Wright put Megan's work on display, she included an arrangement of live flowers in a vase, the reproduction of the Renoir work, a palette with paint and brushes, a photograph of Megan working on her painting, and a typed paragraph dictated by Megan about her work. Many children and teachers in the building were able to see Megan's painting and the display. While it is recommended that educators do not assign copy-work to children, Megan's "copy-paint" was clearly her own idea; Mrs. Wright's encouragement allowed Megan to explore color mixing on her own terms. (See color Plates 1–8 for this and other examples of Megan's artwork. The color plates are accompanied by brief discussions of the artworks using the language of art explained in Appendix B.)

While Megan was painting the picture of flowers, other children were using different kinds of art media to make their own pictures of flowers (see Figure 5.3). Some children used paper at the discovery table to create collages. For example, Caleb twisted paper to represent the stems and leaves of his flowers. He drew different sizes of ovals, circles, and squares to represent the petals of the flowers.

PROVIDING IN-DEPTH EXPERIENCES WITH NATURAL MATERIALS

Mrs. Wright wanted to give the children more in-depth experiences with flowers. She had heard the children talking about the flowers growing along the edges of the playground. The next time they were outside, Mrs. Wright and the children walked around, looking at some of the flowers.

One of the children asked, "Where do flowers come from?"
Mrs. Wright said, "They were planted in the soil."
Tatiana asked, "What is soil?"
Mrs. Wright replied, "It is the same thing as dirt."

FIGURE 5.3 This child found a new way to use her painting. She cut out parts of it to make a collage to show blossoms falling from trees on the playground.

She sat down with Tatiana around one of the flower plants, and they looked at the bottom of the plant. Mrs. Wright told Tatiana that under the ground were the roots of the plant. Tatiana asked, "What are roots?"

Mrs. Wright knew that she had to find some way to help the children understand that a plant was more than stems, leaves, and flowers. A few days later, she brought a pansy plant to school with the flowers blooming and took the children outside to plant it. She and the children used the spades from their sandbox to make a hole in the soil. They talked about the roots, stems, leaves, and flowers on the plant. They dug a hole that was big enough for them to put the roots in and cover them with soil. While digging the hole for the pansy plant, the children discovered the many colors of soil.

> *Lauren:* Look. Where I am digging, it looks orange.
> *Juan:* I am going to dig deeper. (He also discovered that the
>   soil was orange.)

Mrs. Wright moved the children away from the plant to an area where they could dig freely.

> *Mrs. Wright:* What other colors of soil do you see?
> *Billy:* I see brown.
> *Tatiana:* I see black dirt.

The children's excitement for digging and discovering the colors of soil led to rich conversations among them. They used descriptive words to label the texture and colors of the soil on the playground:

> Reddish pink
> Orange
> Wet

Gooey
Soft
Thick
Brown
Black

The teacher brought several baby food jars for the children to use to collect soil. Each time the children collected a sample, they covered the hole before they left. They took the jars with the soil inside to their classroom. Tyler took her jar with soil over to the sink and added water. She chose a paintbrush and stirred the water and soil very carefully; then she got a piece of drawing paper and began moving her brush back and forth on the paper.

She said, "I made a paint. I'm painting with the dirt." She dipped her brush in the mixture of soil and water and painted with the mixture. Other children noticed what she was doing and added water to their jars of soil and began to paint with the mixtures. VyVy had a mixture of orange soil and water. She said, "I'm going to paint a big oval for a pumpkin." Billy made the comment, "My dirt paint is darker than yours." The teacher used this opportunity to teach the children a new word, *soil*. She told them that dirt could be called soil and that they were "soil painting." Soil painting became a popular activity.

Nadia said, "My soil is the same color as yours. No, mine is darker." The children continued to bring in more soil samples the next day (see Figure 5.4). Bobby said to Victoria, "My soil is a red color. I'm going to dig deeper to get more orange dirt." One day when they were outside, the teacher said, "What would happen if you dig over here?" The children found the same colors of soil in other places in the yard.

Later, one child, Lee, picked up a yellow petal that had fallen from one of the flowers in a vase. She rubbed the petal on a piece of paper. She discovered that the petal left a yellow mark. Then she rubbed the petal over another area of the paper and noticed that the petal left a fainter yellow mark. She gathered more petals from different vases and rubbed them on her paper. Excitedly she called out, "Mrs. Wright, come here and see what I did. I made yellow color with yellow flowers and pink color with pink flowers!"

Mrs. Wright asked Lee if she could paint with flowers. Lee immediately gathered more petals and "painted" a design with them. The next day Mrs. Wright and several children brought in flowers from home: dandelions, daffodils, violets, and different colored impatiens. While painting with the flower petals, the children discovered that some made brighter colors than others. Soil and flower painting became popular activities in this classroom.

These are examples of learning what children can do with the natural environment when they are encouraged to explore, experiment, verbalize, and reflect.

FIGURE 5.4 A child collects samples of soil to make new colors.

BUILDING CONCEPTUAL KNOWLEDGE WHILE ENHANCING ART EXPRESSION: THE CITY

In order for children to construct knowledge, they must have experiences in a variety of meaningful situations. For example, children may have a firsthand experience by visiting a part of their own city, or if they live in rural or suburban areas, a nearby city. They can also use secondary resources such as the library, Internet, postcards, photographs, maps, and videotapes.

Before she began the theme "The City," Mrs. Platt, a first-grade teacher, did her own research about the city. She looked at national and state standards for art and other subject matter areas. She read research articles, talked with her peer teachers, and interviewed the community leaders in the town. Mrs. Platt identified three primary goals:

1. The students will be able to identify the key features of the city.
2. They will identify the importance of community workers.
3. They will work with various art media to express their concepts about the city.

In order to begin the topic, Mrs. Platt decided to use a KWL chart to identify "what we *k*now, what we *w*ant to know, and what we *l*earned." She asked the children to come to the large open area in the middle of the room where they could move freely. She began by asking, "Where are we going next Thursday?"

> Colin said, "I know. We're going to the city."
> "That's right," Mrs. Platt replied. "We're going to have a tour of the downtown area of our city. I want you to think of the characteristics of a city." She continued, "What do you think we will see in the city?"
> Johnny replied, "Big, tall buildings."
> Morgan asked, "Are there any short buildings in the city?"
> Mrs. Platt asked, "What do you think?"
> "I think there must be," said Morgan.

Mrs. Platt recorded the children's ideas about their city, and organized them in the form of a *web*. (A *web* is a schematic map—a graphic organizer where the topic is written in the center and related words are written around it.) She wrote the word *city* in the middle of the web. Around the word *city* she wrote *tall buildings*, and then she wrote, *short buildings*.

> Jimmie said, "I live in the country. There are not many police-men in the country, but I think there are a lot of policemen in the city."
> "Why do you think there would be more in the city than in the country?" asked Mrs. Platt.
> "There are more bad things that happen in the city," said Pako.

Mrs. Platt wrote *policemen* on the board.

> She asked, "What do you mean 'bad things happen in the city'?"
> Jimmie replied, "I mean there is more stealing and more shooting. You know, there are more people."
> Then Mrs. Platt asked, "Are any police women?"
> Juan said, "A police lady came to visit the school."
> Mrs. Platt said, "Yes, she did. There are men who are police officers and women who are police officers."

(Depending on their background, a few children may be afraid of police officers. Teachers should not be surprised if a child shows anxiety at seeing the police.)

> Mrs. Platt asked, "What else do you think about when you think of the city?" The children continued to name the things

they thought they would see in the city. Mrs. Platt asked, "How can we find out if these things are part of the city?"

Thomas said, "Well, we can do research."

Julie said, "We can go to the city. When we go, we will see some of these things."

Most of the children thought that the research would help them learn more about what they might see in the city. As part of their research, a few children brought in postcards and photographs of cities, reproductions of paintings of cities, and videotapes of cities.

Mrs. Platt told the children that they could use geometric pattern blocks to show what they had learned through their research. The children worked by themselves or in small groups to create visual representations of their ideas. They made a variety of two- and three-dimensional constructions with the geometric blocks. Monica made a fountain with blue blocks rising above the foundation of the fountain.

Juan: Monica, what are you making?

Monica: Look. This is how I am going to show water.

Juan: How do you know that there are fountains in the city?

Monica: I saw fountains in a picture in the book about cities.
    I know we'll see a water fountain.

Mrs. Platt overheard the conversation. She said, "We have to wait until we go to the city to find out if there are fountains there." Another child, Billy, made power lines.

Mrs. Platt: What shapes did you use to make the power
    lines? Are all your shapes the same?

Billy: No, I made poles out of square blocks, and the power
    lines I made out of rectangular blocks.

Mrs. Platt: In what directions do your lines move?

Billy: I used two long, straight blocks for the power lines.
    They are horizontal lines and move this way (*he pointed to
    the blocks*). And I used rectangular blocks to make the
    poles. They make vertical lines. Up and down lines.

Mrs. Platt: What do you think would happen if there weren't
    any power lines in the city?

Billy: Gosh, I don't know. I guess we wouldn't have any
    lights. And the people couldn't watch TV.

Line is a design concept woven throughout the visual art curriculum in many art programs. Billy and his classmates had learned about line directionality with the art specialist in their school. It appears that Billy transferred what he learned in art class to his understanding of power lines. The children had also learned the words *horizontal* and *vertical* in mathematics, and Mrs. Platt had asked the children to place their papers (not art) vertically or horizontally.

Mrs. Platt asked the children to draw the placement of the blocks on paper. Some children carefully picked up each block, placed it on the paper, and traced around it; others looked at the pattern blocks and visually transferred what they had made to the paper.

Exploring the City

During the tour of the city, the children took in the sights and pointed out their observations to each other. They listened to the sounds of the city and mimicked them. Mrs. White, a tour director for the city offices, told the children and adults about the city buildings and the people who worked in them. The group went to the rotunda of City Hall, where the children touched the toes of a large sculpture. They noticed lines and shapes in the city's architecture and touched the ridged surface of the metal poles of the streetlights. They also toured the art gallery.

Myla: That painting looks like Vincent Van Gogh made it because the paint is so thick.

Mrs. Platt: Do any other paintings remind you of other artists we talked about in class?

Peter: Yes, this one looks like the way Mr. Matisse cuts out shapes and glues them for his pictures.

Morgan (after saying that she was going to draw buildings in the city): I am going to draw some little and some big.

Mrs. Platt: Why do you want to draw buildings that are different sizes?

Morgan: Because some look big and some look small.

Mrs. Platt: What do you mean, Morgan?

Morgan: Well, when something is up close it's small, and when something is far away it's big.

Mrs. Platt understood that Morgan was beginning to notice the difference in scale, or relative size of objects, as they are perceived from a particular perspective. She said, "Morgan, look at the building at the end of the block. Does it look big or small?"

Morgan: It looks kind of small.

Mrs. Platt: Now look at the building in front of you, Morgan. Does it look bigger or smaller than the building at the end of the block?

Morgan: It looks gigantic.

Mrs. Platt asked Morgan how she might represent what she had perceived, in her artwork. "Morgan, can you think of a way you can make your artwork show the other children what you noticed about the sizes of buildings?"

> *Morgan:* Oh yes. I can paint buildings that are big shapes
>   and small shapes.
> *Mrs. Platt (probing Morgan's ideas about buildings)*: Which
>   buildings would be far away from you? The buildings
>   painted with big shapes, or the ones painted with small
>   shapes?

Mrs. Platt made a mental note to talk with Morgan as she painted her representations of buildings, and later to have her share her discovery with the rest of the class. This is an example of the use of a ZPD. Mrs. Platt knew Morgan had difficulty understanding perspective. She took advantage of this opportunity to assist Morgan in her understanding of size changes from foreground (near: bigger) to background (far: smaller).

Representing the Experience

When they returned from the city, the children discussed what they had seen. They reported on how their observations differed or matched their predictions. Several children talked about the big buildings, the loud noises, and the colorful artwork they had seen in the art gallery. Billy realized that the power lines he thought he would see were not there.

> Mrs. Platt asked, "Did we see any power lines today? What did
> Mrs. White, our tour director, say about them?"
>   Billy answered, "That they were trying to bury them."
>   Mrs. Platt asked the children what other things about the
> city had surprised them.
>   "It's very noisy. There are lots of cars, and all the cars
> are going real fast."
>   Beth said, "I heard this train go by, and it sounded real
> loud. I thought it was going to run over us."
>   Sheila responded, "Oh you silly, it couldn't run over us.
> It was at the end of the street. It looked little."
>   Beth asked, "Can we make pictures of what we saw?"

Mrs. Platt asked the children to look around the room at the different kinds of art media. She had planned for the children to use the art materials to represent what they had learned. They could compare these representations with their earlier predictions and research about the city. In addition, Mrs. Platt had given the children time to experiment and explore with various art materials prior to this field trip. Mrs. Platt asked the children how they might represent the noise of the city in a picture. "I could show people screaming and yelling and laughing at the cars," said Terry. Dwayne was intrigued with the largeness of the toes on the sculpture in the City Hall rotunda when he looked up at them. He said he wanted to draw a picture of the toes.

> Mrs. Platt asked him, "What materials would you use?"
> Dwayne responded, "Crayons."
> Mrs. Platt asked Dwayne to think about how he would show the bigness of the toes. "Will you draw yourself looking up at the big toes? Will you use bright colors to make the toes stand out?"
> Dwayne said, "I have to think about it."

After the children had completed their artwork, Mrs. Platt asked them to write a sentence about their illustrations. Then they gathered in the circle, and told about their artwork. Through listening to each other's ideas about the city, children can refine and extend their own ideas. The Vygotskian approach stresses that children learn new information through verbalization with their peers.

> *Tatiana:* I drew a store.
> *Mrs. Platt:* What shapes did you use to show your store?
> *Susan:* I drew a big square for the window.
> *Mrs. Platt:* I see you did. The windows in my house are small, and the square window in your drawing is big.
> *Billy:* I thought I would see power lines in the city, but I didn't.
> *Mrs. Platt:* Yes, and what did Mrs. White tell us about the power lines?
> *Billy:* That they were burying them. So I drew cars.
> *Suzie:* I see a green car in your picture. My mama has a green car.
> *Timmy:* The cars were noisy.
> *Mrs. Platt:* How did you use your art materials to show noise?
> *Timmy:* Some of the people are screaming and yelling, and some of them are laughing at the cars.
> *Mrs. Platt:* Sharon, how can you see the noise in Timmy's artwork?
> *Sharon:* Because I see stoplights, cars, and lots of things.
> *Maria:* The city is busy.
> *Amy:* I drew the city busy with lots of cars.

Another child, Tony, painted trees and stores. Mrs. Platt asked Tony how he showed houses in his artwork.

Tony: On top of the stores.
Mrs. Platt: Were there a lot of houses in the city, Tony?
Tony: Yes, there were.

Later the children painted pictures of the buildings in the city. They placed their paintings on the walls outside of their classroom so that their school-mates could see them (see Figure 5.5).

Constructing a City in Three Dimensions

The teacher wanted the children to have the experience of construct-ing their city in three dimensions. She posed the following question: "Boys and girls, we have lots of art pictures to show our ideas for the city. When you make pictures, you work in two dimensions. You can show how tall and how wide something is. But when you want to show how thick or how deep it is, as well as how tall and wide it is, what materials could you use?"

The children answered, "Modeling clay," "blocks," "wood." Mrs. Platt asked, "Remember the big sculpture we saw in the rotunda at City Hall? How was the sculpture different from the paintings we saw, John?" John answered, "We walked all around it, to see it all." Mrs. Platt continued, "Remember how we use blocks to build? When we do this, we are building structures in three dimensions. We show how tall and how wide and how thick or deep our block structure is. And we can walk around the structures we build with blocks. Can we walk around our drawings to see how deep they are?" The children replied "No" and asked if they could make their city in blocks. Some days earlier, Mrs. Platt had asked the children and their parents to bring in small boxes, paper towel tubes, juice cartons and their caps, and an assort-ment of found objects such as buttons, parts of toys, scraps of wood, fabric, and yarn. These items had been placed on the discovery table for the chil-dren to manipulate. Mrs. Platt now reminded the children about the collec-tion and suggested that they use what they had brought in. The children knew that they had access to foil and cellophane paper, along with construction paper, paint, and other art materials in the room. She encouraged them to experiment with the materials and to draw plans for their structures.

Later, the children made a three-dimensional city from the boxes and other art materials. They made a school, a gas station, a library, and an apart-ment house. To utilize parent involvement, Mrs. Platt gave the children an assignment to complete with their parents: The children and parents used small boxes to build models of their own houses. These were placed with the city at one end of the classroom (see Figure 5.6). When the principal saw the city, he asked the class to put it on display in the school library.

Collaborating with the Art Specialist

When Mrs. Platt read the story *Citybook* (Rotner & Kreisler, 1996), the children became curious about cities at night. They were struck by the

FIGURE 5.5 This class exhibited its "city" artwork on the hall bulletin board.

phrase, "City night, city light," and by the images of silhouettes of buildings with lights and streetlights. One child said, "O-o-oh, that is so neat!
Can we try to make our own city pictures at night?" Mrs. Platt asked the
children how they might represent their city at night. They brainstormed
how they might represent the city buildings and lights. The children suggested that they use dark blue or black construction paper. They thought
they should use colored chalks for the lights and glitter for the stars. One
child asked the class, "Remember when we made the mural of a city in art
class? We used fluorescent crayons." Another child added, "We punched
holes in our building shapes too."

   When the children in Mrs. Platt's first grade recalled what they had
learned in art class, and applied it to their classroom city project, they were
integrating concepts and skills into a whole learning experience. They were
using artistic thinking in an authentic creative problem-solving context.
Earlier in the school year the art specialist in the school had introduced
the students in Mrs. Platt's class to the way artists show foreground, middle
ground, and background in their two-dimensional work. They had looked
at different ways artists depicted cities. They had talked about how artists
use art media to express ideas about cities. For example, action lines, bold
shapes, and bright colors show the "busy-ness" of cities in works by John
Marin, Joseph Stella, and John Sloan, contrasted with the loneliness and
isolation of cities shown in Edward Hopper's works. The art specialist in
this school presented art content and taught the children art skills and

FIGURE 5.6 The students are constructing their city in three dimensions, using cardboard boxes and other materials they have collected from home.

concepts. The classroom teacher gave the children the opportunities and guidance to explore ideas further through content-related studies of interest to the children. (Collaborations are explored further in Chapter 7.)

The principal in Mrs. Platt's school was exceedingly pleased with the results of her collaboration with the art teacher. He understood that, as a result of this collaboration, Mrs. Platt was reinforcing what the art teacher was doing, just as the art teacher was reinforcing what the classroom teacher was doing, and remarked,

> I'm real impressed with the way the art brings the academic subjects alive. It makes things so much more meaningful, and I am seeing how the integration of the subjects just makes the learning so much more enjoyable and relevant. I can see the transfer of the students' knowledge and how they can see the artist in themselves.

DOCUMENTING CHILDREN'S LEARNING

One of the advantages of choosing a topical theme is that it becomes a catalyst to involve children in extensive art explorations. One of the best ways to help children understand that they can express themselves through art is to take photographs of them as they actively participate in firsthand experiences. For example, after a group of 4-year-old children ran around the trees on the playground, made leaf angels, picked up sticks and other nature items, they noticed the leaves turning yellow. Their teacher, Mr. Sloan, took a photograph of three girls using the leaves as umbrellas. He took notes of his conversations with the children, and their conversations with each other. He continued to take photographs to use to document the children's firsthand experiences.

When they came inside, the children enthusiastically began using the art materials to create leaf pictures. Mr. Sloan listened carefully to the children's conversations as they made their pictures. Hoang painted a tree.

> *Christina:* Leaves are falling off your tree because the strong wind was blowing.
> *Hoang:* Well, what happened to our elm tree?
> *Christina:* The leaves changed color.
> *Manuel:* All of the leaves fell off the tree.
> *Zachary:* And then they blew away. I'm going to make fast lines to show them blowing away.
> *Aaron:* I saw a tree with no leaves. It's not as pretty as my tree. I used the shapes for my leaves.
> *Zachary:* Because the leaves fell off.
> *Manuel:* I'm making lots of trees. I put my leaves on the ground and used straight lines for the limbs. They are colored leaves.
> *Aaron:* Because they change colors.
> *Christina:* Because they change like a rainbow.
> *Zachary:* The clouds were moving away.
> *Manuel:* Because the wind was blowing them. The elm tree is cold. It doesn't have any leaves on it anymore.
> *Pamela (painting with the white paint):* I'm making winter.
> *Zachary:* It's not winter, but your picture looks like winter.

Mr. Sloan continued taking photographs of the children as their pictures changed.

> Hoang held up his painting for the children to see. He said, "Look, I show us walking in the leaves."
> Manuel said, "I put a lot of leaves in my picture. Look at my pile of leaves."
> Hoang placed his picture next to Manuel's and said, "Let's put our pictures together. My children can go into your picture and play in the leaves."
> Manuel replied, "That's a good idea."

Mr. Sloan was surprised that Hoang had thought of putting his and Manuel's picture together. He did indeed have a good idea. This is an example of children reflecting on their ideas, talking, and working together to extend and refine concepts they have learned through firsthand experiences. They felt comfortable in their environment, and therefore were confident in making decisions about their artwork and developing their ideas.

The children continued talking about the elm tree as they mixed tempera paints by pouring the primary colors, white, and black from cups into separate, small baby food jars. Mr. Sloan wanted to capture their art experiences by taking photographs and making notes about the children's conversation during the art process. He made notes on the materials and processes the children used to make their pictures. Jamie painted pumpkin seeds with a feather, and glued them on her picture of the tree.

Teachers need to pose questions that will reveal the children's thinking about their work. For example, Mr. Sloan asked Jamie, "What colors do you need to make your paint?" Jamie replied, "Yellow and blue." The notes Mr. Sloan took provided him with ongoing dynamic assessment of Jamie's knowledge and her ability to represent these concepts through art media. Jamie said, "I want to make dark green paint." Mr. Sloan asked Jamie to name a dark color. She replied, "Maybe black." He suggested that she add the color black to the green paint to find out what would happen. Jamie discovered that adding black paint made a darker shade.

Mr. Sloan knew that he would be unable to capture every child's conversations in his notes on this particular day. He kept careful notes to assess what the children said, and took pictures of the art processes they used. Mr. Sloan had worked with these children over the past year, and had become more aware of the significance of keeping careful records of what they said and did. He assessed each child's work over a period of time, and used this information to plan appropriate activities for the children.

Mr. Sloan had the recent photographs enlarged, and chose a few to put on a project display board as documentation of the children's experiences. The child-child and teacher-child conversations were typed on a word processor in a clear, bold font. These typed conversations were attractively mounted along with the photographs of the children's outdoor experiences and their artwork. The project display board included the work of 10 different children, and was entitled "Four-Year-Olds Investigate Leaves and Trees."

Documentation is time consuming; however, the advantages make the effort worthwhile. Well-documented, attractive panels are seen by everyone in a school—children, teachers, visitors, school staff, and parents. When display boards are placed in the classroom, children quickly notice them. Large- and small-group discussions around display boards provide the children with opportunities to reflect on their past learning (see Figure 5.7).

Documentation of children's work and transcriptions of their conversations can be displayed on a hall bulletin board. Ms. Ramos read the story *The Mitten*, by Jan Brett (1989), to her first-grade students. The children made a model of the story covering the science table with a white sheet and cotton batting. They made small animals, trees, and people from various materials. The children wore their own mittens as they each told portions of the story from the model. Another familiar story, *The Three Little Kittens*, was read and compared with *The Mitten* by constructing a Venn

FIGURE 5.7 A photograph captured this child's expression. He is intent on what he is drawing.

diagram. To integrate mathematics, the children hung pairs of drawn mittens on a clothesline strung across the hall bulletin board. The Venn diagram, pictures made about the story, and stories written by the children about the story, were displayed under the clothesline of mittens.

Mr. Larkin introduced the theme "Winter" by taking the second-grade children outdoors after a snowfall. This led to explorations with snow, ice, and temperature. Throughout the study, there were several panels created and displayed to illustrate the conceptual understandings of winter. The panels of snow experiences were mounted attractively on construction paper frames. Mr. Larkin, who had no hall bulletin board, attached long sheets of colored craft paper to the walls. In spite of the fact that he had to improvise, the children's work was always on display. Artwork, photographs, and children's written work can be exhibited in attractive and creatively appealing ways. (Different ways to display artwork are found in Chapter 2.) One teacher highlighted the monthly themes in her classroom and arranged them on display boards. At the end of the year, she chose several artifacts from the individual boards and displayed them in a yearly time-line fashion.

Display boards and bulletin boards call attention to both content and the aesthetic aspects of the children's work. This form of documentation makes visible the children's learning and the processes of their art experiences from beginning to end. Documentation serves as a communication tool between teachers, children, and parents. Attractive bulletin boards encourage school personnel, other children, and parents to stop, look, read, and react to the many investigations, ideas, and art experiences children have had (see Figure 5.8).

FIGURE 5.8 The principal and teacher discuss the child's representation of a story.

USING PORTFOLIOS FOR ASSESSMENT

An art portfolio is a purposeful collection of children's artwork. It may include children's completed work or works in progress. Transcriptions of the language used by the children to discuss their artwork may accompany it. The portfolio provides children, teachers, and parents with a picture of where the children were when the collection was begun and where they are at present. This helps to inform the teachers as they plan for the children.

The portfolios can be made from large brown envelopes, two pieces of tag board stapled together to create a pocket, or even large pizza boxes donated by a local pizzeria (see Figure 5.9). The portfolio can be personalized with the child's photograph and/or a drawing or design created by the child. Children enjoy decorating their portfolios with a variety of materials. The children's portfolios should be kept at school and accessible to the children. Portfolios can be shared with parents to discuss their child's growth in art expression. Because young children want to take their artwork home, some teachers help children select the work to save in their portfolios. Other teachers may scan, photograph, or make color copies of artwork to put on exhibit or save in children's portfolios.

We encourage teachers to use the Art Portfolio Assessment Scale (see Appendix A) and Art Talk Checklist (see Appendix B) about every two months to evaluate the children's artwork, art vocabulary, and art concepts represented visually and verbally. Teachers should also encourage the children to evaluate their own artwork. For example, first-grade children drew pictures to illustrate their ideas about flower gardens. Then they went

FIGURE 5.9 A local pizzeria has donated pizza boxes for this class's portfolios.

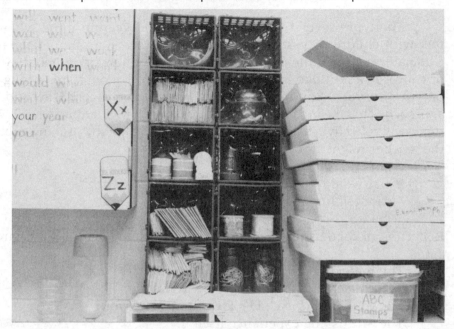

outdoors to observe a butterfly garden. They drew the butterfly garden while sitting close to it. They compared their earlier drawings with their observational drawings. All of the students realized that their second, observational drawings included more details about the garden: Earlier flowers were stereotypical in form and color, while closely observed flowers varied in size, shape, and color; insects were included, and some children drew the school building behind the garden.

State and Local Standards

Standards are the learning goals usually set by the state and local school districts that communicate to teachers the skills and concepts children must learn by the end of a school year. Often state standards reflect national standards for the subject areas. We asked a third-grade teacher, Mrs. Pender, "How do you implement the district standards with the art experiences you plan for the children?" She answered, "That's easy," and quickly produced a copy of the Reading and Language Arts standards. She chose one of the children's art portfolios, and reviewed the work samples which included drawings, paintings, collages, and photographs of three-dimensional work. She read a standard and checked it off whenever the artwork reinforced the standard. She said, "See, I can use the portfolio to assess how each child is developing. For example, this child's painting is an illustration for the cover of a book report. It represents the main idea of the story and includes many details about the central character."

Portfolio Interviews

There are several things teachers should keep in mind when they talk with children about their artwork. First, teachers should always include affirmation of the child and his or her unique work when they begin or conclude a portfolio interview. "I know you worked hard (a long time) on your artwork. You must be proud of your hard work." Second, good approaches to take include the probing approach (Schirrmacher, 1997) and the use of reflective dialogue (Taunton, 1983). Using the probing approach, the teacher might say:

> What would you like to say about your artwork?
> Please tell me more about it.

Reflective dialogue stresses asking questions about the following areas:

> The materials and processes used in the artwork
> The child's choices in imagery and medium
> The sources of the child's ideas for the artwork
> The art making experience itself

Third, open-ended questions are best (Sparling & Sparling, 1973). Avoid questions that require merely "yes" or "no" answers; these questions are best followed by "why" questions, like "Why do you think that happened?" Briefly, there are six categories of questions that seem most appropriate when talking with children about their artwork. They are questions about

1. *Process:* How did you make your artwork (painting, picture, sculpture, collage)?
2. *Materials:* What materials (or tools) did you use?
3. *Ideas:* Tell me about your idea(s).
4. *Knowledge* (concepts, vocabulary, artists studied): What kinds of shapes did you use? Did you use shapes like Matisse?
5. *Reflection:* What do you like best in your artwork?
6. *Future:* What will you make next? Do you want to add anything to this artwork?

Appendix B includes a summary list of suggestions to use when talking with children about their art.

When teachers interview their students, they notice that their students become more confident in art making and more articulate in their art talk. Mrs. Keen said that her previous, untrained comments to her second-grade children about their artwork tended to be repetitious empty praise: "That's wonderful." "How interesting." "I like that." When she reflected about her comments, she realized that the children must have had no idea what was wonderful or interesting, or what she really liked about their artwork. Mrs. Keen's reflections motivated her to put more thought and effort into her comments. She began to be more specific in her comments and used art vocabulary as she pointed to particular aspects of their work. As Mrs. Keen developed her interview techniques, she noticed that her students tended to mirror her questions; they began to interview each other about their artwork:

> How did you make that?
> What is your idea?
> Can you show me how to mix green?
> Your painting looks like Monet's.
> I like the way you mixed white to make a blue tint there.

Mrs. Keen also realized that the children were not only mimicking her interviews, they were also addressing the language arts standards as they talked:

> They asked appropriate questions.
> They were able to focus on specific topics.
> They were able to present information to others.

CONCLUSION

The importance of children's language and child-child and teacher-child dialogue is discussed in this chapter. To enhance children's artistic expression, teachers must ask open-ended questions and listen to children's comments about their artwork. It is through questioning and exploring ideas with children that teachers guide their students' learning processes and art expressions.

The zone of proximal development and dynamic assessment are strategies to use to improve children's learning as teachers recognize what children can do now, with assistance, and what they will be able to do later, independently. It is hoped that teachers will view dynamic assessment as part of their everyday planning and teaching.

Often teachers neglect to incorporate the immediate environment in their teaching. This chapter shows teachers how to take advantage of what is close at hand to help children understand their school environment. A theme, "The City," was presented as one in which teachers can combine learning in all subject areas, including visual arts. In this unit, art experience became a vehicle for developing concepts and learning skills.

Documentation is a valuable way to record and present information. Children's art activities and representations of their artwork can be shown in carefully designed panels. The collection of art materials found in each child's portfolio can provide teachers, parents, and children with evidence to use for ongoing assessment.

Children learn language skills by using their teacher's interview techniques in their conversations with each other:

Phillip: I made a sun.
Joan: Tell me more about the sun in your picture.
Phillip: I put it in the grass, because the sun is going down
        to the earth.

6 Children Learn About Artists and Themselves as Artists

> Mrs. Miller, an elementary school art teacher, received a post-card from one of her students who was vacationing with his family in New York City. They had visited the Museum of Modern Art, where Colby found an art postcard he wanted his art teacher to see. Colby's mother carefully wrote his dictated message:
>
> > Dear Mrs. Miller,
> >   I went to Jackson Pollock's art store in New York. I think you knowed some pictures in there.
> >   Love, Colby King

Earlier in the school year, Colby and his kindergarten classmates had become interested in Jackson Pollock's artwork after they had seen a reproduction of one of his paintings in the art room. They made comments such as "I think this art looks like 'scribble-scrabble'" and "It looks like my little sister made it." Mrs. Miller and the kindergarten teacher, Mrs. Moore, planned to build upon the children's interest. The art teacher told Mrs. Moore about an art activity she did when second graders studied the artist; she used marbles dipped in paint, which the children rolled on paper placed in a shirt box, creating paintings in the style of Pollock. Mrs. Moore borrowed the Jackson Pollock reproduction and a children's book about the artist, *Jackson Pollock*, by Mike Venezia (1994). She read the book that evening and selected passages she would read to her students.

PAINTING IN JACKSON POLLOCK'S STYLE

The next day Mrs. Moore brought several kitchen gadgets to school: an eggbeater, a turkey baster, a toothbrush, a pastry brush, a squirt bottle, an eyedropper, and a spoon. Mrs. Moore used these items as props when she read about the artist's processes. The children enjoyed the story and were excited about the novelty of the painting tools to "splatter and fling" paint. They especially related to Jackson Pollock's frustration with drawing things exactly as he saw them and with his feeling that he could not draw as well as other artists. The children experimented with these tools and the primary colors on individual papers, critiquing themselves and each other as they worked (see Figure 6.1).

> *Larry:* Look, the egg beater made green with the blue and
>   yellow paint.
> *Greyson:* May I borrow the turkey baster? I like the way it
>   squirts the paint. It sounds like "splopp"!
> *Sal:* Greyson, your painting looks pretty good just like that.
> *Rosa:* See the yellow bubbles I can make with the eyedropper.

The children asked if they could make a large splatter painting together, making a mural on the floor, just as Jackson Pollock had done in his barn. A parent offered to supply the 6' by 10' canvas cloth. One child brought in the art history textbook her father had at home, and pointed out a photograph of a Pollock painting. A visitor videotaped the children painting in Jackson Pollock's style.

The children donned raincoats and galoshes to paint their Pollock mural (see Figure 6.2). A custodian offered to build a wooden frame to stretch the canvas in order to hang it on the wall. After the mural was complete, the children invited their art teacher, Mrs. Miller, to view the mural and to join them in watching the videotape of them painting it.

> *Janelle:* I remember slinging the red paint.
> *Sam:* Look. Dylan's using an egg beater.
> *Thomas:* See how the turkey baster shoots the blue paint all
>   across the cloth.
> *Marie:* Mr. Pollock splattered the paint because he wanted
>   to paint his own way, because he couldn't paint like
>   other people.
> *Carlos:* He stepped on his paintings. We did too.
> *Conner:* He used a lot of colors.
> *Andie:* He used his imagination.

Mrs. Moore asked the children to look at their finished mural and talk about how it looked to them.

> *Julie:* I think it's pretty. I like the colors.
> *Dylan:* The painting is unbelievable.
> *Aleesha:* I see a centipede over here.
> *Marie:* Here is a candy cane.
> *Dylan:* I see a backwards E up at the top.

Other children saw basketball hoops, tree roots, a swing, dinosaur, yellow spotted cow, swimming pool, tornado, fishing pole, and more letters of the alphabet. At each answer, Mrs. Miller asked the children to explain what

FIGURE 6.1 "This is my Jackson Pollock painting for my portfolio."

it was about the colors, lines, or shapes in the painting that gave the children these ideas. She would say, "Pretend I cannot see this painting. Tell me more about those lines." She would ask questions like, "What does that shape suggest to you? Have you seen something like that before?" She helped the children find descriptive words, adjectives, and metaphors to verbally express what they perceived in the work. In this way she helped them to better understand the relationship between media, tools, and the images or ideas they might represent. To synthesize their visual and verbal artistic experience with their mural, Mrs. Moore asked the children to suggest titles for the work. Some titles suggested were the following:

> *Splatter*
> *Super Action*
> *The Rainbow*
> *The All Different Kinds of Things*
> *The Kindergarten Painting*
> *Seek and Find*

INTRODUCING ART REPRODUCTIONS TO CHILDREN

As the previous section illustrates, children are interested in looking at works of art, and often identify with the artists whose art resembles their own. They enjoy the cutout shapes and bold colors seen in Matisse's work,

FIGURE 6.2 Children enjoy using Jackson Pollock's painting techniques.

Van Gogh's bright colors and thick paint, Pollock's nonrepresentational art-work and his approach to painting through action movements and nontra-ditional tools, and Monet's outdoor scenes that are light and airy. They enjoy trying to decipher the mystery of the abstract art of Wassily Kandinsky, Franz Marc, and Paul Klee. They enjoy seeing Romare Bearden's collages, and learning about African American subject matter and themes (see Figure 6.3). They identify with the images and content in Faith Ringgold's story quilts, and can appreciate Ringgold's combining of descriptive writing with the images in her story quilts. In addition, children are familiar with Ringgold's book *Tar Beach* (1991), and can identify with the central character, Cassie, who can own something she wants by flying over it in her imagination.

The Work of Faith Ringgold

A second-grade teacher, Mrs. Raven, became interested in the artwork of Faith Ringgold. She showed the children a photograph of the artist and introduced her as a sculptor, collagist, quilt maker, painter, and writer of children's stories. "Those are all the ways she creates pieces of art." When

FIGURE 6.3 The teacher is careful to select art reproductions from a variety of cultures. This multicultural perspective also attends to racial and gender balance.

Mrs. Raven mentioned that Ringgold was born in 1930, Howard asked, "Is she old?" Mrs. Raven asked, "How can we tell how old she is? She was born in 1930. This is 2000." Ben said, "She's 70. Is she still living?" The young teacher answered, "Yes, she is. My grandmother is 70 and she's alive."

Mrs. Raven continued, "I have a picture here of one of Faith Ringgold's paintings. It shows a quilt story. She tells her stories with pictures instead of words. What do you think about it? Tell me what you notice."

Sam said, "Everybody, they wearing church clothing."

Howard said, "She used shapes, like squares and circles."

Mrs. Raven asked Howard, "Can you show us one?"

Howard walked up to the print and pointed to a square shape and a circle. He added, "There are lots of circles."

Mrs. Raven asked, "What shape has four sides and four corners?"

Howard answered, "A square can be a rectangle."

Suzanne added, "I see a lot of circles."

"Where?"

"On the plates."

Mrs. Raven then asked, "Tell me what you notice about the colors."

"Rainbow colors."

"Light colors."

"Dark colors."

"Beautiful colors."

Mrs. Raven asked, "What kind of colors are they?"

"Warm colors and cool colors."

"What are the cool colors?"

"Green. Blue."

Mrs. Raven continued to probe, "Look at the outline. What do you notice about it? Faith Ringgold put the pictures in the middle. She painted the center. The outside is fabric."

Howard summarized his interpretation of the artwork, "I think that she went to church, and they had a picnic and she is telling a story about it."

June said, "I know what she's saying in the picture. I think she's doing a wedding."

Mrs. Raven asked, "Why do you say that?"

"Because everyone is dressed up and there's a cake in it."

Mrs. Raven added, "So just like when we tell stories with words, we can tell stories with pictures; when you look at this picture you can interpret the story for yourself. Would you like to see some more paintings by Faith Ringgold?"

Extending the Children's Awareness of Ringgold's Art Work

Mrs. Raven used technology to show more of Ringgold's artwork. She had created a Power Point presentation, using the television monitor to show the children several more story quilts. She asked the children, "Do you see any similarities between this quilt and the others?"

Janelle: It has Black people, just like the other one did.

Ben: It has pretty colors.

Mrs. Raven: Think about how it is the same and how it looks like a quilt. What story do you think she's trying to tell? She's drawing, painting, and writing about people she knows . . . just like you do.

When the teacher showed Ringgold's *Mother's Quilt*, the children were curious about the title of the work. The teacher explained that some artists keep some of their artwork and sell others or perhaps give some to their friends. Mrs. Raven said, "But she didn't give this one away. She kept this one. Why do you think she kept it?" Several children guessed.

"It may have been one of her favorites."

"She made it when she was a little girl."

"It might be her favorite quilt."

Mrs. Raven asked, "Why do you think a quilt called *Mother's Quilt* might be one of her favorites?"

"Because she might have made it for her mother."

Mrs. Raven said, "Now I'm going to show you another story quilt. This one is called *The Dinner Quilt*. Do you think that's a good title? Why?"

"There's food on it."

"What story do you think she's trying to tell?"

"A story about when they eat at the table."

"Is that what you think Faith Ringgold had in mind? Who's in the picture?"

"Black people."

"Who do you think they are?"

"Their family."

"Yes. When you write stories, do you write about strangers, or do you write about people you know?"

"People we know."

"So it's probably her family or friends or cousins or teachers. Would you like to do things in your art area related to things you know, like Faith Ringgold did? (See Figure 6.4.) Think about the times you spend with your family and friends at home and at school. Try to remember as much as you can to tell your story. Choose the art media that will help you tell the story. Later I'll read aloud the story *Tar Beach* which Faith Ringgold wrote and illustrated."

In this vignette, Mrs. Raven used technology to extend the children's awareness about Faith Ringgold's creative work. The children were already familiar with Ringgold's illustrations in her book *Tar Beach*. Mrs. Raven found more of the artist's work on the Internet and used Ringgold's "story quilts" as slides in a computer Power Point presentation displayed on the television monitor in her classroom. Mrs. Raven helped the children explore various meanings in the visual imagery of Ringgold's story quilts. She also reinforced the children's understanding that visual images can symbolize ideas and feelings, just as words do in written stories.

CHILDREN IDENTIFY WITH ART REPRODUCTIONS

A first-grade teacher, Mr. Goldman, placed near the housekeeping area a brightly colored Matisse painting, *Harmony in Red*. The print showed a woman placing fruits on various shaped containers. The children did not comment on the Matisse print until Mr. Goldman brought in real fruit and containers. He placed the fruit on a table beneath the print and observed the children as they played with the fruit. He asked, "Do you think this vase will hold an apple and an orange? How many pieces of fruit do you

FIGURE 6.4 This child is placing his story drawing on the class's Faith Ringgold–style story quilt. (Photo courtesy of *The Herald*, Rock Hill, South Carolina.)

think this container will hold? Could you put these apples in this container?" Then he said, "What is the lady in the painting doing with the fruit?" They talked about the woman in the Matisse print arranging the fruit on a plate. Then they arranged some of their fruit in a similar manner (see Figure 6.5). Later, they painted pictures of their still-life arrangements.

Although teachers may display a print related to a theme of study, occasionally children will show little interest in a reproduction. Perhaps the print's two-dimensionality, small scale, and, if laminated, the smooth shininess of its surface might all be distractions to a child. During a farm unit, a preschool teacher placed a reproduction of Sully's *The Torn Hat* at eye level. The painting is of a child wearing a farmer's bonnet. The children ignored the picture throughout the unit. However, the next year, several children commented on the child's hat.

LEARNING FROM MONET'S PAINTING *THE BRIDGE AT ARGENTEUIL*

Ms. Brighton, a preschool teacher, held a framed 16" × 20" reproduction of Monet's painting *The Bridge at Argenteuil* for the children to see. This painting had been in the room for several weeks; it had been hung on the side of a bookcase, at the children's eye level, but no child had commented on it to Ms. Brighton.

She said, "I have a painting to show you today. Have you seen it before?"

FIGURE 6.5 These children arrange food in various containers while discussing a reproduction of a Matisse still life. They are reflected in the mirror behind them.

"I have seen it one hundred thousand times," Newton said. "I have that picture in my house and my Mommy painted it." (Indeed, the teacher had seen the print of the Monet painting in Newton's home when on a home visit.)

"Let's look at this picture. Where have you seen it in the classroom?"

Newton said, "Over at the other art table."

Ms. Brighton continued, "I want to tell you more about this picture. An artist painted this picture, and he has a name. His name is Claude Monet. Say his name with me."

"Claude Monet."

Ms. Brighton asked, "Do you know some other artists?"

Ashley said, "Matisse."

Abbie added, "Van Gogh."

Ms. Brighton said, "Yes, that's right."

Newton said, "I already painted a picture like that, but it doesn't have people, and it doesn't have that bridge."

Pointing to his picture, Ben said, "I put skies, trees, and boats in my picture."

Brittany said, "I see an animal in the clouds."

Ms. Brighton asked, "What kinds of animals do you see in these clouds, Brittany?"

"A caterpillar."

Ms. Brighton said, "Look at the colors Monet used. Tell me about them."

Ben said, "White and blue. He used blue for the water and white for the clouds."

Marta added, "There is green and yellow in this part. And some brown, orange, and white."

Noticing Tints and Shades

Ms. Brighton asked, "What are some other colors you see in the picture?"

Meg said, "Light blue."

Several children began to talk at once. Ms. Brighton said, "Let's listen to Meg's idea. Meg, what do you mean a 'light' blue?"

Meg said, "It's a kind of light blue."

Ms. Brighton said, "I wonder how Monet makes colors that he uses to paint light colors."

Several children responded, "He mixes colors!"

Ms. Brighton asked, "Well, what would he need to mix? You know Monet was one of the painters who like to paint outdoors. He wanted to make the sky in this painting light blue like the sky he saw. How do you think he made the sky in his painting light blue?"

Newton answered, "He mixed white with blue."

Ms. Brighton said, "We would call that 'making a tint.'"

Katelyn said, "I see something else. There's a black boat."

Ms. Brighton asked, "Katelyn, what do you notice about the colors Monet used? Do you see any dark colors in his painting?"

"Black."

Ms. Brighton said, "Monet had different shades to make it dark. How do you think Monet made dark shades of colors?"

Allyson said, "Mix red and purple to make it dark."

The children are relating this information to what they had done previously at the art table, when they were mixing paints.

Ms. Brighton said, "Tell us some of your ideas. Melanie, remember how you wanted to make navy blue? What did you do?"

Melanie said, "I added black to blue."

Ms. Brighton said, "That would be making a shade of a color. Do you think Monet has mixed colors to make shades and tints?"

The teacher is applying vocabulary in the context of experience.

"What does the artist want us to see in the dark green paint?"

Jay said, "That little boat looks like it is sinking."

Ms. Brighton said, "I think Jay has made a good observation with color. He thinks this boat looks like it is sinking. Jay, did Monet use blue and white in the water? It's hard to distinguish between the colors of the water and the boats, isn't it?"

Experimenting with Colors

Ms. Brighton continued, "Listen. At the art table today we have some red, yellow, blue, white, and black paint. I want you to use these colors to paint a picture."

Toby said, "We need white so we can make it light."

Ms. Brighton said, "See what you can find out at the art table. I'm going to take this picture and hang it back on the wall in the art area."

In addition to small cups of the paints, the teacher had available various-sized paint brushes and paper for the children to use. She placed the Monet painting in the art area. The children went to the art table and began experimenting with the paints, stirring them carefully.

Ms. Brighton asked, "What kind of shades and tints will we get?"

Jay used a spoon to spatter paint to make grass. He said, "Look what my spoon can do."

Toby said, "See what happens when you pour the white in the paint."

Ms. Brighton said, "I see lots of ideas at your table. Ben, you added the yellow to the black. It makes the black lighter. It looks kind of greenish now."

Brittany said, "I need some green."

Ms. Brighton asked, "What do you think you will need to make green?"

Brittany said, "Red and blue. I need some blue."

Morgan said, "That doesn't make green."

Ms. Brighton said, "Morgan, what makes green?"

Morgan looked at Brittany's paint and said, "You need to add some yellow to your blue to make green. See, this is how you do it."

Victor said, "I made gray with black and white. Come see my gray."

Portia said, "I'm playing in the water. See the water picture?"

Ms. Brighton said, "I see water in the picture. What else do you see?"

Portia said, "A boat."

Extension Activities

Ms. Brighton continued to refer to the Monet painting in the art area. Morgan looked over at the painting and said, "I see another boat in the water." The teacher realized that the child saw the reflection of the boat in the water. She talked with the children about how much the reflections looked like the objects they reflected. The teacher extended the children's experiences later on in the day, by taking them outside to find other reflections. They saw a reflection of a cloud in a mud puddle and the trees' reflections in the windows around the school. Containers of water were placed outdoors so that the children could see the reflections of the sky, clouds, and trees. One child shouted, "I can see myself in the water!"

These extension activities gave the children a better understanding and appreciation for the Monet painting, and encouraged them to investigate reflections in their environment. These are excellent examples of integrating science and art.

MATISSE'S SPECIAL NEED AND HIS PAPER CUTOUTS

Children are interested to learn that a number of famous artists have had disabilities to deal with. When the painter Henri Matisse became ill and was too infirm to paint standing in front of an easel, he changed his working process and medium. Confined to his bed or a wheelchair, he began to make large collages with shapes he cut out of papers that had been painted by his studio assistants. When children begin their art experiences by exploring paper, they can become very interested in a photograph of Matisse sitting in his wheelchair, holding a piece of paper in the air and cutting it with scissors. They see that the desire to make artwork can overcome a disability.

ART AND CHILDREN WITH SPECIAL NEEDS

Many early childhood classrooms include children with special needs. These children may receive special assistance in their regular classrooms or in resource rooms that they visit for part of the day. We encourage classroom teachers to help them express their ideas and feelings with art media. Often the biggest obstacle to fulfilling their potential for children with special needs (or any child) is the lack of opportunity for creative expression. The following examples show how teachers can provide such opportunity to children with a range of special needs.

Children with Attention Deficit Hyperactive Disorder (ADHD)

James entered first grade in the middle of the year. His teacher, Ms. Martinez, observed James's impulsive behavior. For example, he looked for a certain yellow pencil for at least 30 minutes, although his teacher told him that he could use any pencil. He brought extra clothes in a book bag and changed them several times throughout the school day. Ms. Martinez referred James for a complete psychological evaluation.

Although his impulsiveness interfered with his learning, James was able to focus on cutting out shapes from paper and gluing collage materials on paper. However, James wanted his artwork to be as he envisioned it. When it was not, he would destroy his work by tearing it and throwing it away. Ms. Martinez reassured him, "It is all right the way it is." Her assurance did little to change his behavior. She cut out freeform shapes for him. He seemed pleased that his teacher also enjoyed cutting out shapes, and he pasted them on his paper. Ms. Martinez modeled appropriate behavior for this child. Since he enjoyed art, the teacher chose art as one way to help him focus his attention on a task.

In formulating James's zone of proximal development, Ms. Martinez defined his upper level: Ask, instead of scream, for help, and stay on task for 5 minutes. When he screamed for help, she said to him, "I can't help you until you stop screaming and ask me for help like this: 'I need help.'"

She planned to concentrate on his involvement with art. In the beginning, the only way this child would focus was when the teacher sat beside him and worked with him. She talked with him about the materials he used in his collage. After a few days had passed, the teacher observed James staying involved with the collage materials for longer periods of time.

Once the psychological evaluation of James was completed, the school psychologist diagnosed him as having Attention Deficit Hyperactive Disorder (ADHD). As a result of the diagnosis, the teacher, parent, and school psychologist created an Individual Education Plan (IEP) for James. His physician prescribed medication to help him deal with the hyperactivity.

For the remainder of the school year, Ms. Martinez encouraged James to use other art media. Gradually, he began to paint at the easel for long periods of time. His learning style was congruent with the IEP, which stated that he needed hands-on visual activity and movement for learning. His teacher kept this in mind as she continued to assess this child's progress and help him reach the upper level of the ZPD. Eventually he began to ask for help and show less frustration in daily tasks.

Another child, 7-year-old Mark, would hide things in his classroom and was reluctant to go outside with the other children. He was preoccupied with his own thoughts and ignored by the children. Therefore, he became a loner. Mark had no IEP, and the teacher, Mr. Evans, had referred him for testing. Mark was seeing a neurologist who had diagnosed him as ADHD and prescribed Ritalin for him. Often, the Ritalin was not effective.

Mr. Evans engaged Mark with other children in marble painting. The children would dip marbles in paint and put them on a sheet of paper placed inside a box lid. One of the children would take one end of the box, and the other child the other end. They would move the box very carefully back and forth to make a design on the paper. The children chose the color of paint they wanted to use and talked with each other about how they would make the marbles roll in the box. This activity helped them learn to cooperate with each other because they had to move the box carefully to control the trail of the paint.

Mark also engaged in what the children and Mr. Evans called "arm dancing," an activity in which the children intertwine their arms with others while holding brushes in their hand and paint together. Mr. Evans taped long pieces of paper on the table top and encouraged the children to paint together with large brushes on the paper while they listened to bright, upbeat music.

In the discovery center, Mr. Evans displayed reproductions of well-known paintings and often discussed them with the children. They learned about the artists, about their history, and about their style and techniques of working. They learned whether or not the artists used bright colors and bold strokes, or perhaps paper and scissors like Matisse. The children made remarks like, "Well, that doesn't look like a Jackson Pollock painting," or "Mr. Matisse used bright colors like that," or "Van Gogh put the paint on his canvas pretty thick." The children became aware of these different techniques because they had been discussed with them.

Mark would look at the artwork and say, "You know, I think I can use my imagination and try to do something like this artist did." One day, Mark painted a picture and said, "This is a Jackson Pollock." He proudly stood next to the Jackson Pollock reproduction and placed his picture beside it as Mr. Evans took a photograph of him. When his painting was admired by a visitor, Mark told her, "Look. I made a Jackson Pollock. See, I splattered all of these colors over my picture. There's blue and yellow over white just like he did." This was the first time that Mark had shared a picture with anyone but his teacher. Through other art activities, he learned to use various types of art media. His relationship with the other children improved. Later, he had an IEP, which also helped the teacher in planning his ZPD.

A Child with Visual Impairment

Billy, a 4-year-old, is partially blind and wears glasses. Because he had vascular albanian disability, the IEP requirements were to wear a cap, sunglasses, and sunscreen outdoors. He could not work near bright light. He had to sit close to objects he explored and needed materials that were colorful so that he could visually distinguish between objects.

At the beginning of the school year, Billy drew people by placing their eyes in the top corners of each side of the paper. He also used the whole paper to make one face. He did this over and over. He distinguished among skin color by using a variety of multicultural crayons representing individual children. His papers representing individual children, resembled a book, and he referred to each page with the name of the child in the class. He showed his book to Mr. Burton, his teacher, who said, "Tell me about your pictures." He would rush up to the children and show them his book. Mr.

Burton often commented, "Look, boys and girls, at the artwork our friend has done."

Mr. Burton encouraged Billy to share his artwork during group time. In particular, the children commented on the eyes. Sometimes they said that the eyes looked funny because they were far away from the nose. However, they liked to have their picture drawn. He continued to draw pictures of children in his classroom. Then he became interested in cutting shapes out of different kinds of paper. Children in the group remarked, "You made a picture with your shapes." As an outgrowth of cutting shapes, Billy became interested in building with blocks and began working with the other children in the block center. The children admired his ability to use blocks to build the streets and neighborhood to illustrate Halloween Safety. They understood that he had eye problems and frequently remarked to the teacher that Billy needed to sit close to them during group time. At the end of the school year he continued to enjoy experimenting with art media. He cut and named shapes and was able to represent concepts with paint.

A Child with Hearing Impairment

Jon had a hearing impairment and wore hearing aids. In order for him to hear the voices of his classmates and teacher in a group situation, Mrs. Hagins wore a frequency modulation device, a microphone clipped to her collar. Her voice was sent directly to Jon's ears. For 45 minutes each day Jon received instruction from a resource room teacher. However, Mrs. Hagins had the major responsibility for Jon and for overseeing his IEP.

Related to Jon's hearing problem was his speech problem. It was difficult for him to express himself, but he was able to verbalize about art. The art helped him to express his thoughts and say what he was trying to get across to the children. He liked art and said he wanted to go to the art area every day. He told Mrs. Hagins, "I want to be an artist so that I can make a lot of money and be a superstar."

A Child with Cerebral Palsy

Bonnie had cerebral palsy and very weak muscles. Her teacher, Ms. Novak, chose activities for her that would involve manipulating materials such as play dough and Legos and peg boards. These materials seemed to be effective tools to develop her fine muscles. Ceramic clay was especially effective because of its plasticity in contrast to plasticine or modeling clay which often needs to be warmed by squeezing to make it workable enough to respond to a child. Instead of expending her energy to make the plasticine workable, Bonnie enjoyed the immediacy and malleability of the ceramic clay. With collage, she was able to express her imaginative ideas by assembling and arranging precut paper and found materials. Ms. Novak used a tray to hold Bonnie's art materials and tools so that they would not roll onto the floor while she worked.

Children Learning English as a Second Language

Roger, a preschool Vietnamese boy, lived with his mother, father, and grandmother. They spoke Vietnamese at home. Because of language differences, his teacher, Mrs. Griffin, found Roger's development difficult to assess. His classroom behavior was disruptive. Mrs. Griffin noticed Roger at the art table using large pieces of paper and crayons. When he realized that she was looking at him, he took crayons and vigorously covered a whole piece of paper with fast lines. Then he looked at her for approval or disapproval. She responded to his gestures by saying, "I see you used a blue crayon and moved across the paper with fast lines." Since Mrs. Griffin gave Roger positive reinforcement while he was engaging in art activities, he experimented with various kinds of art media.

It was difficult to determine to what extent Roger's disruptive behavior was a result of his inability to use English. Art became an outlet for the child. At the art table he could tear and cut paper, use crayons vigorously, and paint swiftly with large brushes. Mrs. Griffin wanted him to use the materials less aggressively and to represent his ideas in a more appropriate way. Through her encouragement and praise, Roger's aggressive behavior improved. Mrs. Griffin's strategy was to ask him to share his artwork during group time. She asked questions about Roger's art processes. "What materials did you use?" "What did you do first when you made your collage?" "Tell us more about your collage." Although Roger sometimes acted silly when he described his artwork, this attention was a positive experience for him. When his grandmother came for him, he often said, "Look at my picture. I told about it." Roger spoke limited English by the end of the year.

Another Vietnamese child, Minh, had lived in the United States for 4 years. This 5-year-old boy had a 16-year-old sister who was encouraged to speak English to him. Therefore, he had some understanding of basic English. On a home visit, his sister acted as an interpreter for the parents and his teacher, Mrs. Cohen. She noticed that a print of a Monet painting hung on the living room wall, and that Minh had paper and crayons and felt pens for drawing.

Minh appeared to understand directions in the classroom, but Mrs. Cohen noted that he followed the lead of the other children when transitions were necessary. He was shy at school, probably because he could not verbally communicate with the other children. Mrs. Cohen introduced him to the papers on the discovery table. He explored the papers for several days before cutting or pasting them. He was delighted with the texture and color of the different kinds of papers. Mrs. Cohen used this opportunity to name colors for the child. He repeated the names of the colors as he heard them. In a short time he could name black, white, blue, and red. He drew pictures with contrasting colors that enhanced his ideas. On a field trip he saw a Dalmatian dog, and when he returned to school, he eagerly used black, brown, and white crayons to draw the dog with the black spots.

Using the Art Talk Checklist and the Art Portfolio Assessment Scale (see Appendices A and B), Mrs. Cohen determined that Minh was advancing quickly in art expression. She planned activities within his ZPD to encourage him to include more than one or two well-drawn objects in his picture. She identified his independent level as drawing one or two objects in a picture without using expressive language. She wanted him to use words to describe what he had drawn. She defined his upper level to include more details in his pictures and to verbally describe his ideas. She used dynamic assessment to formulate plans and assess his progress. Gradually he began to mix well with the other children and learn English words and verbal expressions from them. Whenever he hesitated, a child would say, "Give him time to think."

Mrs. Cohen knew that although Minh's English was limited, he needed the same kinds of experiences as the other children. For example, she took the children outdoors to observe caterpillars. She encouraged Minh to watch the caterpillar's movements, notice the colors, and to look at her as she repeated the word "caterpillar." She hoped that he would talk about the caterpillar when he drew it. Using this strategy, the child learned many new words. He became confident with his artwork and wanted to share it with the other children while he was drawing and during group time. He would frequently say, "Hey, look at my picture." By the end of the year, he was using a variety of art media to express his ideas, and began to verbally express these ideas to the other children.

ENJOYING EACH OTHER'S ART

Children like to hear about art from other children's perspectives. Sharing art in a group setting gives them an opportunity to reflect on their own and other's art experiences (see Figure 6.6). In the following example, 7-year-old Harry was showing the group the picture of a fish he had drawn. Marla spoke up and said, "You need to draw some more water for your fish to swim in." The group sharing continued:

> *Sara:* Teacher, can I show my collage?
> *Mrs. Bridges:* Yes, let's listen to Sara talk about her collage.
> *Sara:* See. I have a row of colored squares on the bottom. They are red and blue paper squares. On the next row I used brown paper towels for the squares.
> *Mrs. Bridges:* Sara, are you finished with your collage? I see some space at the top that you haven't used.
> *Sara:* I know. I would like to use some buttons to make the rest of my collage.

Later that day, Sara added colorful buttons and broken pieces of chalk, placing them in the squares in a one-to-one correspondence. When the

FIGURE 6.6 Children enjoy talking about their artwork.

group met again, Sara proudly showed her finished collage to the group. When Matthew saw Sara's collage, he said, "I like those colors."

> *Terry:* Sara, you made a pattern.
>
> *Mrs. Bridges:* Tell me about the pattern you see in Sara's collage.
>
> *Terry:* See. A circle, square, a circle, square, a circle, a square.
>
> *Mrs. Bridges:* Does anyone else see another pattern in Sara's collage?
>
> *Gene:* I see a big button, a little button, big button, little button, big button, little button.
>
> *Mrs. Bridges:* All of the patterns go around the picture.
>
> *Shelby:* Your collage makes me think of Matisse.
>
> *Mrs. Bridges:* Shelby, why does Sara's collage make you think about the artist Matisse?
>
> *Shelby:* Because Matisse has lots of shapes and colors in his pictures.
>
> *Mrs. Bridges:* Yes, and Henri Matisse liked to make patterns with his shapes and colors. You are all like artists, aren't you? Some of you sign your name like the artists do.
>
> *Paul:* Can I show my picture? I made straight lines, zigzag lines, and free-form shapes.
>
> *Mrs. Bridges:* Tell me about free-form shapes. That's a new word we learned.
>
> *Paul:* They are not like a square or a circle, or a triangle. They can be any kind of shape.

Mrs. Bridges: Where does your red zigzag line end? (Paul pointed to the last line in his picture.)

Mrs. Bridges: Paul, did you use any white lines on your picture?

Paul: No. If I used white lines, you couldn't see them because the paper is white.

Mrs. Bridges: Are your lines curved?

Paul (pointing to the curvy lines): These are curvy. They touch other lines, and they make free-form shapes.

This dialogue shows how children often apply mathematical understanding through art since patterning is an important activity in mathematics. In addition, young children are taught the concept of pattern in art.

Seeing other children's artwork helps them to express their experiences through visual representations. For example, in a first-grade class, Becky showed the children the picture she had drawn of a squirrel. The squirrel was drawn at the top of the paper and a house was drawn at the side of the paper.

Jasmin asked Becky, "Why don't you draw a tree?"

Then Mr. Taylor asked, "Why do you think she should draw a tree?"

Jasmin said, "Because you see squirrels in a tree."

Mr. Taylor asked, "Where do you see squirrels when we are outdoors playing?"

Tommy said, "Sometimes you see them running on the ground. Becky could draw the grass in the picture."

These children gave Becky ideas to include in her artwork. If they had not had outdoor experiences, these children would not have had the prior knowledge in offering their ideas for Becky's artwork (see Figure 6.7).

Group sharing, whether in a large- or small-group setting, gives children an opportunity to show their artwork to each other, giving them a purpose to use art language, extend their ideas, and to practice using art vocabulary with one another. They learn that there is more than one acceptable way to show ideas with art materials. Listening to others' suggestions may help them to improve not only their artwork but also other areas of the integrated curriculum. This can happen in any classroom where children feel safe and secure and learn to appreciate one another's work.

WORKING WITH ARTISTS

Another opportunity to enrich the child's understanding of the art world is provided through collaborations with professional artists. Local artists can help bridge a gap in young children's understanding between

FIGURE 6.7 These children are aware of art in their daily lives. They are mixing paints to paint pumpkins outdoors.

their own art and the art they see in a book or museum, as illustrated by the following example.

Peggy Rivers is a professional artist whose paintings are on exhibit in an art gallery in the town where she lives. Several teachers arranged to take their students to visit the art gallery. The artist agreed to talk with the children in the gallery, and she invited the children to visit her studio afterward. Buses were reserved to transport the children from the school to the gallery, then to the artist's studio, and back to school again. Some parents accompanied the children.

When they arrived at the gallery, the children ran excitedly from painting to painting. They pointed to things they "saw" in the abstract paintings. One painting in particular caught their attention. Children said they saw mushrooms and strawberries in it. They also saw a chicken leg, chocolate cookies, and fish on a plate. They all agreed that they certainly saw food in this painting. Peggy Rivers confirmed that indeed she had been thinking about food when she painted the work, and invited the children to find the pear she had hidden in it (see Figure 6.8).

Peggy Rivers talked about her life and work as an artist. She helped the children interpret deeper meanings in her paintings. She explored the children's ideas as she told them about her intentions in the paintings. She said, "When I make these paintings I try to put my thoughts about the universe in them. I love colors and I love the stars. I like the purple and pink together. I try to make my thoughts real when I paint."

Peggy Rivers tried to model talk about art from a professional artist's perspective. She explained to the children how when they make art, they

FIGURE 6.8 A child and an artist share ideas about the painting.

are making visual images of what they are thinking about. When the artist spoke about collage, the children understood, because they had made collages in their classroom. When the artist tried to explain how she makes "the universe on a cellular level," the teacher helped to "translate" her words to the children's developmental level by relating this vision to what they see in the microscope in their classroom.

When the artist asked the children what they like to draw and paint they answered, "houses," "space ships," "sunshine," "rainbows," "robots," and "hearts." One child answered, "I like to draw pictures of me." The artist asked, "What are you doing in the pictures?" The child answered, "Playing."

When another child said that she likes to draw her family, the artist asked, "What are they doing in your pictures?" When another child answered, "Trains," the artist asked him where they were going. In this way the artist prompted the children to think about more than isolated images in their drawings, and to expand their ideas to include their thoughts about the action, context, or environment.

While in her studio, the artist showed the children her very large brushes. She showed how she attaches canvas to the wooden frames called "stretchers," which stretch the fabric taut. She showed the children how she mixes paint to get the colors she wants to use. She told the children that she likes to mix her own colors, to invent new colors, just as the children do in their classroom.

The children were delighted to hold various brushes and other painting tools, to learn the proper names such as *canvas, stretchers, tube wringer*, and *palette knife*. They looked at her sketch book and saw that she sketches her ideas to develop and save them. She shared that she likes to listen to music when she paints, and that this makes her so happy that sometimes she dances to the music as she paints. They were intrigued with the range of paintings on her studio walls, from realistic to abstract. They saw the paintings as actual objects, not simply prints or reproductions in books. Their visit helped to bridge the gap between what the children see in a book or museum and their own art making. They realized that artists are real people, just like they are.

CONCLUSION

This chapter illustrates the interest children show in the work of artists. When children become familiar with artists and their work, art becomes real to them. They learn that different media and techniques are used by artists to obtain different effects. They can become totally absorbed in painting in a manner similar to that of Jackson Pollock. They can see similarities between their art processes and the collages of artists like Henri Matisse. Children also identify with artists whose illustrations appear in children's books, such as the painted story quilts of Faith Ringgold.

Teachers' familiarity with artists allows them to use art reproductions in a purposeful way in their classrooms. They can ask meaningful questions and guide children's comments and insights about their own and other's artwork. Such questions, comments, and insights can motivate children to act on art media to express their own ideas. Talking with each other about their ideas gives children an appreciation of each other's efforts, and the opportunity to use art language. Children also appreciate knowing about artists' lives and the media, tools, and techniques they use. Children enjoy learning that artists come from various backgrounds and diverse cultures, and that artists may be found in the communities in which they themselves live. Sometimes children even aspire to become professional artists after they have learned about them.

> *Child:* I'm going to be an artist when I grow up.
> *Teacher:* Why do you want to be an artist?
> *Child (very confident and sure of herself):* Because I know how to do things.
> *Teacher:* What kind of artist are you going to be?
> *Child (pauses, then speaks thoughtfully):* A painting artist.

7 Collaborating with Parents and Colleagues

When June shared her artwork with her teacher, Ms. Burton, she said, "You can have my pictures. My mother doesn't like my pictures." At Thanksgiving, after a visit to a turkey farm, June made an unusual representation of a turkey with sawdust shavings from the workbench. She glued the sawdust to a piece of wood that resembled the form of a turkey. Then she colored the turkey with magic markers. She made a border with sawdust around the turkey and colored the border green after it had dried. She gave Ms. Burton the artwork to take home with her. She said, as she often would say, "Put it in your bedroom."

When June's mother came to get her daughter that day, Ms. Burton told her in private about the artwork that June had just completed, and that June always asked Ms. Burton to take the artwork home. Ms. Burton said, "If you don't want it, I'll take it. But I think you should look at it. It's very unusual." The mother replied, "Oh, is art work important? I keep telling June we don't have room at home for it. I have to keep throwing it away." When she looked at the sawdust turkey plaque, she was very surprised and said, "We'll take that home with us." From then on, June took her artwork home where it was displayed on a bulletin board.

About 15 years later, Ms. Burton was standing on the playground and saw a young woman she thought she recognized. As the two approached each other, the young woman said, "Hello. Do you recognize me? I'm June, and I was one of your students. You liked my artwork. I'm in college now. Can you guess what my major is? Art!"

INVOLVING PARENTS IN ART EXPERIENCES

Parents are a valuable resource for facilitating children's learning. To reach out to the parents of the children in her kindergarten, Mrs. Miller gave a presentation for them at the beginning of the school year on the topic "What is Child Art?" She discussed her philosophy and goals for the children's art. As a result of this discussion, the parents began to appreciate and understand their children's artwork in a new way.

It is also effective for teachers to send newsletters home to the parents each week. Children's drawings can be photocopied to include in the newsletters, with examples from each child's artwork chosen throughout the year. Supplying extra copies of the newsletter allows parents to send it to relatives.

Parent Support for Art Activities

Teachers with limited budgets for art supplies may find parents very responsive to requests for donations. At the beginning of the year, Mrs. Davis placed a tree limb in a large, tall flowerpot to use to communicate with parents of her third graders. She attached colored-paper leaves to the limb and wrote on the leaves descriptions of materials the children might need during the year. She asked parents to bring in items like buttons, keys, bags, eyedroppers, magazines, old calendars, greeting cards, Polaroid film, and a plant. The parents were encouraged to take a leaf home until all the leaves had fallen off the tree. The notes to parents became icicles in the winter and green leaves in the spring (see Figure 7.1).

In one classroom, parents, along with the children, were involved in the maintenance of the art area. Parents restocked the art area with supplies from the teachers' supply room. This helped to keep materials on hand and organized. Some parents brought in boxes of paper from their homes, offices, and businesses. Scraps of paper and other classroom materials were saved by the children to use in many art projects. Gift wrap, ribbon, and yarn were favorite recycled materials for artwork. One child discovered the utility and beauty of using discarded paintings to cut out shapes and glue them on her collages.

In another classroom, an inventory was sent home to the parents to determine their interests and hobbies. For example, one father made birdhouses and volunteered to make a birdhouse with the children. Several mothers enjoyed growing and arranging flowers. They brought flowers to school and arranged them for the children. Later, the children were given flowers to arrange. Children worked in small groups or individually, arranging the flowers in baskets, vases, and dishes. Often, they painted or drew pictures of their arrangements.

Sharing Art Experiences with Parents

There are many ways that teachers can share the children's art experiences with their parents. Children and teachers in Oakwood School created an art museum. Children's artwork was framed and mounted on classroom walls. During the year, children's artwork centered around a particular theme of study, such as animals of the rain forests, farm life, or

FIGURE 7.1 This teacher has used construction paper leaves on a tree branch to communicate her wish list to parents.

favorite authors' books. In addition to the classroom, the exhibit was displayed in the foyer of the building.

Parents can be involved in participating in school projects. For example, the parents and children together made models of their homes for the unit on the city that was described in Chapter 5. They chose the materials to make their homes from items they found at home. The parents were invited to see the final production of the city in the school library.

Another project involved the music from *Carnival of the Animals*. The children drew pictures of the animals and moved to the music to describe their animal's movement. For the final production, parents, grandparents, siblings, friends, and the principal sat around the room and enjoyed the children as they moved to the music dressed in self-made costumes. The children's pictures and written descriptions of their work were displayed on trifold project boards (see Figure 7.2). Some of the remarks made by the visitors were:

> "I didn't know Sara could do that."
> "Look at John's picture. It looks like he was listening to the music."
> "Look at what my brother made."
> "Look at Morgan's tiger."

The first-grade classes in Woodland School collaborated to present stories during a Storytelling Day. Parents, family members, and friends were invited to participate in the event. The children planned the dialogue to

FIGURE 7.2 This child proudly points out his ideas about fish, displayed on a trifold board.

role-play the stories, made costumes to depict the characters in the story, and painted their scenery. Through the stories, they interrelated art, reading, speaking, listening, and writing. The stories were presented by groups of children at 12 stations, and the parents moved from station to station to enjoy the stories.

Videotaping is an excellent way to share with parents whose schedules make it difficult for them to visit the classroom. With the money from a grant, Miss Whittier made videotapes of the children engaged in art and other activities. At midyear, the children took the tapes home so that the parents could view them; and at the end of the year, videotapes were taken home to be permanently kept by the parents. These videotapes provided a record of the child's activities during the year.

Through effective communication, parents can participate in the art experiences of their children and support teachers in their integration of art into the curriculum.

COLLABORATING TO PROVIDE QUALITY EXPERIENCES IN VISUAL ARTS

As mentioned in Chapter 1, both NAEYC and NAEA recommend that young children have daily opportunities for artistic expression and be offered a variety of media, tools, and techniques in order to express and represent their ideas and feelings through the arts. Further, it is recommended that beyond the preschool years, children experience the arts as an explicit focus in addition to their integration into other areas of the curriculum. Through these experiences, children should acquire fundamental concepts and skills in the arts.

Colbert and Taunton (1992) present three major needs that must be met to insure that young children receive quality art instruction: Children need many opportunities (1) to create art, (2) to look at and talk about art, and (3) to become aware of art in their daily lives. Such opportunities can best be provided through the collaboration of art specialists and classroom teachers who appreciate the value of creative arts experiences for young children.

The *National Visual Arts Standards*

As stated in the *National Visual Arts Standards*, "Creation is at the heart of this instruction" (NAEA, 1995, p. 15), when young children are involved in media, tools, and processes as they explore their world through opportunities to create. They develop manual dexterity with tools and materials as they develop and refine their ideas and feelings. They learn to make choices about media and techniques as they examine and discuss their own art work and that of others, including the artwork of their peers as well as that of "other people, times, and places" (p. 15).

Among the six content standards of the *National Visual Arts Standards* (NAEA, 1995) is one that reads: "Making connections between visual arts and other disciplines" (p. 17). Within this content standard, there are two achievement standards for students in grades K–4. Students can

   a. understand and use similarities and differences between charac-
      teristics of the visual arts and other arts disciplines
   b. identify connections between the visual arts and other disciplines
      in the curriculum. (p. 17)

This second achievement standard encourages substantial collaboration between arts specialists and classroom teachers and promotes the concept of integration of learning at the early childhood level.

Using Standards to Collaborate

An increasingly attractive opportunity for teachers to collaborate in order to integrate the early childhood curriculum is being provided through district, state, and national standards. In some districts and schools, teachers are studying their own and other discipline standards to see where opportunities exist to integrate the curriculum.

There are several important things to bear in mind when such collaborative opportunities develop. The first is the intrinsic value of each discipline—those things that each particular discipline has to offer to the whole child's development: linguistic, mathematical, spatial, musical, artistic, and so on.

Second, it is vitally important to maintain the integrity of each discipline: There are skills and concepts in art that we have drawn on throughout this book and discuss further in Appendices A and B. These concepts are understood by and best taught in cooperation with an art specialist, if one is on staff in a school.

Third, children often will naturally integrate disciplines. While art specialists can provide the skills and concepts to express in art, the classroom teachers provide the time and context for the artistic understandings to be applied, for unique and personally relevant artistic expression to occur. They can ask open-ended questions, encourage children's ideas and suggestions, provide a variety of art materials, and allow ample time for children to construct artistic representations of their learning. (Refer to Chapter 5 for the example of collaboration in the "City" theme.)

How does collaboration between art specialists and early childhood teachers begin? Often such collaboration starts when the classroom teacher delivers the students to the art room: The teacher may see reproductions of works of art on display in the art room and ask to borrow particular works that correspond to a unit or concept he or she is planning to teach (see Figure 7.3). The teacher may arrive a few minutes early to pick up the students at the end of class and hear them talk about their work, with the art teacher in critique, or among themselves as they share what they did in art. Or, upon arriving back at their classroom, the teacher may ask the students: "What did you learn in art today? Can you show me what you did?"

Sometimes art and early childhood teachers have the same planning period or after-school duty and find a few minutes to talk about what they are doing. Such occasions to plan together are serendipitous; others may be more structured. Some principals arrange joint planning times to support collaboration and integrate curriculum (see Figure 7.4). One principal designated lead teachers at each grade level, who were responsible for sending information to the art, music, drama/dance, physical education, and other specialists about units and concepts planned for the month's study in the academic subjects. Occasionally principals will provide planning time before the school year starts for early childhood and specialist teachers to collaborate. Some arts specialists take the initiative themselves to distribute their planned themes of study by the month or throughout the year at each grade level.

In a school that does not have an art specialist on staff, early childhood teachers can explore with the principal the possibility of bringing in a consultant in art education. This art specialist could work in the classroom with the teachers or present professional development workshops.

Butterflies: An Example of Collaboration

A first-grade teacher, Ms. Starr, often talks with the art teacher, Mrs. Jones, as she delivers her children to the art room for their weekly lesson.

FIGURE 7.3 The teacher and art specialist select reproductions of works of art for the classroom.

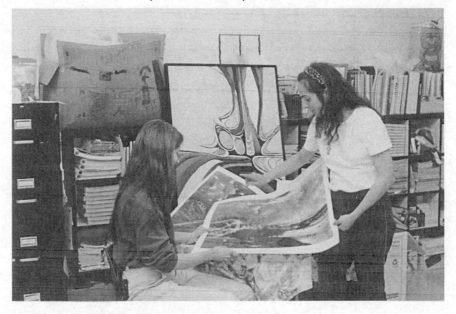

She notices the reproductions the art teacher puts on display, the books and materials she sets out, and the art vocabulary she puts on the chalkboards. Ms. Starr talks with her students when they return from the art room with any art work they may have brought back, "interviewing" (her word) them about the art materials and techniques they used, the artist they may have studied, or book the art teacher may have read to them prior to art making. Ms. Starr is careful not to be judgmental as she talks with students about their work. She avoids using such empty phrases as "That's great" or "How interesting." Instead, Ms. Starr interviews the children about their work, asking them to tell her about their ideas and particular materials they may have used, or to explain a technique to her. She incorporates the language of art, the elements and principles of design, into the conversations.

One day in early autumn, Ms. Starr asked Mrs. Jones if she might borrow drawing boards for the children to use. They were studying insects, and she was planning for them to go outside and sketch in the butterfly garden another teacher had planted the previous spring. Although Mrs. Jones didn't teach an insect unit until later in the year, her curriculum did emphasize the concept of "line" in art at this point. She suggested that Ms. Starr wait a week to borrow the drawing boards so that she could adapt her planned unit to a study of butterflies. Ms. Starr agreed.

Mrs. Jones took out the book *Charlie the Caterpillar*, by Dom DeLuise (1990). She put up several art reproductions that emphasize line, including Kandinsky's *Composition: Storm*, a work in which students could identify different types of lines. She also put on display a reproduction of a

FIGURE 7.4 The principal, the teacher, and the art specialist discuss the children's creative artwork.

photograph of a Seminole councilor's coat, a Native American article of clothing showing perfect symmetry, and a large reproduction of a butterfly. She wrote the following words on the chalk board: symmetry, line of symmetry, straight lines, zigzag lines, dotted lines, wavy lines, curly lines, crooked lines. Her objectives were that the student would be able to

- Define *symmetry*, *line of symmetry*, and *symmetrical*
- Identify straight, curved, zigzag, dotted, broken, wavy, curly, and crooked lines
- Create a paper butterfly that has symmetry and a variety of lines

When Mrs. Jones read *Charlie the Caterpillar* to the students, she drew the different types of lines on the board at the appropriate time (as Charlie encountered different characters, different lines were introduced). Then she had the children interpret the different kinds of lines with their bodies as they listened to a recording of a "butterfly" song. Finally, she distributed scarves for them to interpret the butterfly's movement.

When they returned to their classroom, the first-grade children performed their butterfly dance for Ms. Starr, their classroom teacher. For the beginning and end of the music, they wrapped themselves in their scarves as if they were cocoons. At the conclusion of their performance, Ms. Starr's children "flew" back to their seats. Now they were ready to draw butterflies outdoors.

Through the collaboration of their art and classroom teachers, these students had developed a broader conceptual understanding about the insects, how they might look, how they might move, and how they might be artistically expressed. A few days later, when the art teacher had a planning period, Ms. Starr took the children outdoors to draw. Mrs. Jones used her digital camera to take photographs of Ms. Starr and the children as they drew together so that they could remember and celebrate the experience.

CONCLUSION

This chapter discusses the importance of making connections among disciplines. Today there is so much for children to grasp in our technological society that educators must help them do what they seem to do naturally—integrate subject matter.

When art specialists, early childhood teachers, and administrators can work together, children are supported by the interest of the entire school.

Parents play a vital role in their children's learning experiences, including those in art. When parents work with their children at home and in school, they show enthusiasm and interest in child art. Children feel proud of what they have done and strive to continue to do well.

An example of parental collaboration that had a positive effect on the child is the following story about three artists: Jackson Pollock, Andie, and her father.

Andie was a student in Mrs. Moore's kindergarten class. One morning after they had started to study Jackson Pollock's paintings, Andie's father, a student in graphic design, dropped her off at school with one of his college textbooks. He told Mrs. Moore that Andie had been looking through his art history book and had come across a photograph of one of Pollock's paintings. Andie had pointed out the artwork to her father, and proudly reported that she too was studying Mr. Pollock's artwork in her school. She said, "We are all artists, aren't we!"

8 Reflections

As we stated in the beginning of this book, we want to show how art experiences may be integrated into all subject areas of the early childhood curriculum. We recognize that it is easier to integrate subject areas for preschool and kindergarten than for first, second, and third grades because of the increased demands of schedules. With younger children, large blocks of time can be provided without interruption. However, creative teachers of older children are able to adjust schedules to include art as they integrate their curriculum through theme-based projects.

With this book we have also sought to help early childhood educators use children's language, actions, interests, and discoveries as the basis for planning children's art experiences at the early childhood level. We want to emphasize the importance of listening to what the children say about their artwork and of valuing their ideas and efforts. The more secure children feel in their environment, the better able they are to develop concepts through creative investigation. The discovery table becomes as important as the art table in this regard.

Further, we tried to help early childhood educators develop and implement more effective language as they talk with children about their artwork. As teachers watch and listen to the children as they work with art materials, they become more skilled in the use of effective language, which we call "art talk." They learn to follow the children's conversations about their artwork and engage in dialogue to develop concepts.

Thus we have demonstrated that the three most important factors in the development of the children's art are

1. The use of art talk with the children.
2. Their immersion in in-depth experiences through the integrated curriculum.
3. The provision of choices in art media, independent decision making, and opportunities and time for reflection.

We have the additional goals of helping children enjoy each other's artwork and respond to the aesthetic qualities in their work as they acquire the ability to value and evaluate their own work. When teachers use art talk to guide the children in discussions about art and artists, the children begin to talk about their artwork to each other, discussing their ideas and supporting each other's efforts as their teachers have done with them. Many examples of child-child art talk were presented in this book to illustrate this concept. We continue to support the importance of language as a tool in cognitive development and consider art a language to communicate ideas and feelings.

In this book we showed how dynamic assessment can be used to identify where children are in their artistic development and in their verbal and visual art expression. The Art Portfolio Assessment Scale (see Appendix A) and the Art Talk Checklist (see Appendix B) can help teachers not only determine where the children are in their development, the lower level of the ZPD, but also plan activities that help children move from their lower level to their maximum or upper level of their ZPD.

In order to use dynamic assessment effectively, teachers have to keep and review in-depth notes and art portfolios. They also should use technology (cameras, video cameras, computers, and copiers) to document growth in art and language—graphically, conceptually, and verbally.

We want to emphasize the importance of collaboration between early childhood teachers and art specialists on themes of mutual interest. Examples of such collaboration have been presented in the book. Art specialists who participated in such collaborations note that when the students from collaborating classroom teachers come to them for art class, they appear decidedly well-prepared for discussions about art and artists, with art vocabularies better developed than their counterparts in other classes at the same grade level, and more confident in their own art making during art class. These students do not hesitate to investigate unfamiliar media and processes.

In concluding this book, we want to share the reflections of the classroom teachers, art specialists, and principals who participated in the study discussed in the preface. Using the approaches described in this book, we all experienced the value of integrating art into the early childhood curriculum.

REFLECTIONS FROM TEACHERS

A Teacher of Four-Year-Old Children—Sharon Mitchell

As a teacher and coauthor of this book, this project has been the most exciting professional learning experience I have encountered in my 20 years of teaching young children. Recently, I heard one of my 4-year-olds say, "I want to go to the art center." What a testimony! Throughout this project the excitement for art and learning have continued to spiral. I have been amazed at the ability of 4-year-old children to express their ideas and knowledge using various art media. In my school, teachers, parents, students, and visitors stopped by the bulletin boards in the hall and in my classroom to study the children's artwork and documentation. When they found out that this was the work of 4-year-olds, they were quite amazed and somewhat perplexed. I often heard adults say, "How can a 4-year-old paint such detailed pictures?"

It has been exciting to apply Vygotskian theory as a teaching and learning tool. I have always believed that children construct and reconstruct their own knowledge through active engagement with their environment. Using the ZPD, however, has enabled me to guide children's thinking about concepts and about their surrounding environments more effectively. The kinds of questions I asked children had a significant influence on their thinking and their ability to use language as a mental tool or a thinking tool. Art has been a major catalyst for children to extend and use language. Children consistently asked to share their artwork with others, and I have become much more aware of their independent or present levels and of ways to assist them to reach their maximum levels of development through daily interactions. Teacher guidance is crucial if children are to reach their maximum level of performance.

The children's enthusiasm and excitement for the kinds of art activities they engaged in had a significant impact on their learning. Art has been a natural way to integrate learning in all subject areas. Children illustrated ideas and concepts about science, stories, social studies, and mathematics (see Figure 8.1).

I have discovered that the children enjoyed learning about recognized artists and great works of art such as Matisse's *Beasts of the Sea*. The children made connections to their world through these works of art. They applied concepts about line, shape, color, and texture to their own world and experiences.

It has been wonderful for the children to develop their portfolios that provided documentation of learning. Children enjoyed reflecting on pieces of their own work as well as looking at other children's work. Portfolios included samples of the children's artwork from the beginning of the school year. The scales and checklists used during the year became a part of the children's portfolios. They provided us with valuable information about each child's progress. Children liked to get out pieces of their artwork and talk about them. "Look at this, Mrs. Mitchell. Look, I put the eyes way up here."

The influence of the affective domain for learning was apparent throughout the project. I saw my own enthusiasm for exploring and discovering various kinds of art media mirrored in the children. The environment played a significant role as well.

As a result of my participation in this project, I am a better disciple of Vygotsky's theory of learning and teaching. This project has defined my teaching in terms of applying theory to classroom practice. I have seen firsthand the remarkable growth in art as well as the cognitive growth of the young children I have taught. I am more confident and focused and committed to this pedagogy, and will continue throughout my teaching career to apply and practice the tenets of Vygotskian theory.

A Kindergarten Teacher—Mary Watson

I was very pleased with the direction in which the program went. Watching children get excited about their artwork meant so much to me. One day as we walked through the art gallery and looked at the paintings

FIGURE 8.1 This child's artwork represents concepts she has learned through experience. The teacher recorded her statements and presented them with the artwork.

My pumpkin has alot of seeds. There is a seed pack, with a whole bunch of seeds in it. The seeds are planted under the ground and dirt. The vines are curvy lines.
Melanie   10-29

on display, the children commented, "You know, I can tell that wasn't a Jackson Pollock. She doesn't paint like Pollock did. And look, there's a mother and child–type portrait over there." Their awareness of color, line, and shape and use of these terms astounded me. Besides the fact that they were more willing to participate in art, they became more verbal.

It was wonderful to find children interacting, making comments to each other about their artwork as they were painting, and talking about colors and spending time coming up with new names for colors as they mixed them. It was so exciting to hear them verbalize, to give each other positive feedback such as, "Gee, I really like that blue that you made. What color does it look like to you?" Or, when they look at somebody else's work, "You know, you really took a lot of time to do that." All of these things helped them to learn how to look at artwork and how to evaluate it. I think they put a great deal of thought into their artwork and certainly showed more pride in their finished work (see Figure 8.2).

I think integrated learning is a given in our classroom; it's a fact, that's what we do, it's what we believe for children. But art allowed us to further our goal of integrating learning. Art helped us with literature, with language, with math, with science. When we explored paper in our discovery center, we were doing part of a science unit called "Natural Objects" about different types of paper and other objects. It was so easy to incorporate "Natural Objects" into an integrated approach. When the children were making books, they were talking about the art that they did, and reading stories about the artists. We learned about the artists' lives; we learned about their techniques; we learned about mixing colors—all kinds of learning that probably is not in a typical kindergarten curriculum. The children are using a more critical eye when they examine things, and it is much easier for them to create and to draw because they can look at something and say, "It's just a group of shapes. So how am I going to put these shapes together?"

I think that art techniques become so natural. Yes, I think that from year to year, even with the same materials or the same topics, you change your style of teaching as it relates to your group of children and their needs. I think I use art more now than I probably would have used it before I participated in this research project. Now we talk about perspective; we talk about colors in different ways, shapes, intensities, or values. We use different words that I may not have used with kindergartners before. Now it is much easier for me to incorporate art concepts. I think that I am more willing to do it also. I have always been a constructivist. I wanted children to construct their own knowledge; but knowing more about Vygotsky's theories, I can see that I can be more verbal and give cues and directions when I might have neglected to give assistance in art. Yes, I think we have grown as teachers as a result of these experiences.

A First-Grade Teacher—Tracy Craven

Working on this project has been a very rewarding experience for me and the students I teach. Through the process of learning about art and the connection to other subject areas, I learned that the children were eager to share their artwork and art ideas. We also learned about famous artists and pieces of artwork that integrated with our curriculum. The students were given many opportunities to talk about their art processes and techniques.

The children created art as a means to express ideas, show the knowledge they gained, or enjoy the aesthetics of the work. Their truly hands-on work with art gave meaning to what they were learning. As their hands were busy creating a piece of artwork, their minds were busy analyzing and synthesizing the information.

I have learned how to question and assist the children in a way that enhances their learning and art, rather than dictating how to do it. Each

FIGURE 8.2 *Teacher*: What a good idea to use your art materials in this new way!
 Child: I used my brain. I thought about what I wanted to make.

child has a sense of success when their individual art is just that: individual. No two pieces were identical, very different from giving each child a pattern to follow. Each child felt his or her work was the best because it was individual and not just the copied picture that was colored the best.

The children were able to talk about their art to each other and to me. They talk about their plans for creating art before they begin. They talk to the children near them and to me while they are actually creating the art. They also get to talk about their art when they are finished. The children show their creations to their classmates and tell about the picture or construction, materials used, techniques used, and maybe even a story about the picture. Many times the children would ask to write a story to go with their pictures. Before this program, the children would rarely ask to write extra stories. The children enjoyed comparing and discussing famous artists and pieces of artwork. They would even compare themselves to the famous artists we have studied (see Figure 8.3).

I've seen more cooperation, teamwork; children working together to solve problems. For example, Katelyn discovered that you can lighten a hue of your watercolor paint simply by adding more water. She was happy to show the other children how to do this, and the other children came to her to be taught this skill. Having children come to each other to learn art techniques gave them much more self-confidence; and children felt free to ask each other for help.

FIGURE 8.3 This child enjoys learning about Claude Monet's life. He tried to paint in Monet's style, and his classmates nicknamed him "Tony Monet."

Individuality, creativity, and success are all benefits from our program. The children have ownership over their work and learning because our approach is fashioned around the beliefs of Vygotsky.

The Collaborating Art Teacher—Rebecca Ramsey

Throughout the past 3 years, I have been extremely fortunate to be able to participate in the project to integrate art into the curriculum. I know that as an artist and an art educator, my love and appreciation of art goes without saying. This opportunity to share my love for art with classroom teachers and have them respond in such a positive and enthusiastic manner has been overwhelming.

During the initial year of this project, when these students were in first grade, I worked with their teacher to integrate our curricula as much as possible. For example, when I taught the concept of line and introduced the different types (wavy, straight, crooked, broken, dotted), the first-grade teacher conducted a survey to determine which type of line was the students' favorite. As a math activity, they created a graph of the results. To integrate science as well, butterflies were discussed in the classroom and "butterflies" were created in the art room using different types of lines. Symmetry was a key objective in this lesson.

The first-grade teacher's enthusiasm for reinforcing art concepts learned in the art room as well as her introduction of artists and techniques in her classroom was definitely contagious. Her first graders were given ample opportunities to work with materials and were eager to do so. I believe that their teacher's reinforcement of art vocabulary enabled students to be more willing to use it during discussions in art class. They came into the art room each week ready to talk about art and to create art. Their "art-readiness" really made a difference!

At my schools, I teach all students in kindergarten through fifth grade. Since this has been an ongoing project over the past 3 years, I have been in the unique position of being able to observe the progress of the students involved. The students who began in first grade are currently third graders. I believe that the most important long-term observation I have made during this project is in regard to class discussions of artwork. In each of my second-grade classes last year, there were two or three students who were involved with this project during first grade. These students showed more willingness to participate in discussions of their own artwork, that of their peers, or that of famous artists. This year, I have noticed this trend continuing.

A Second-Grade Teacher—Lynn LeGrand

Before I became involved in this study, I had been uncomfortable with using art materials in my classroom. As my school district had put more emphasis on academics and preparing children for standardized and high-stakes testing, I had not even considered ongoing arts in the classroom a possibility; certainly, I had no room or desire for an art discovery table. However, I did use arts and crafts ideas to help celebrate holidays. Children made pumpkins at Halloween, turkeys at Thanksgiving, snowmen and Santas at Christmas.

But the same year I participated in this study, I was preparing for National Board Certification, and I decided to explore interdisciplinary connections between social studies and visual art. It was November, and I wanted an alternative project for the pattern-turkeys I had had the children do in previous years. I wanted the children to show more original ideas in their turkeys. I wanted them to do research on turkeys and to apply what they learned about real turkeys to their artwork. I spoke with the art teacher, who had several ideas and resources to share with me. I borrowed a large reproduction of a turkey by John James Audubon and put it on display in my classroom. I took the children on a field trip to a nearby turkey farm, where they saw real turkeys and learned how they were raised. I found photographs of turkeys in the state wildlife magazine, and put them on the display board. In addition, I brought in a number of picture books with stories about turkeys and set up a discovery table.

Then I told the children that this year they were to create their Thanksgiving turkeys with their own ideas from what they had learned in their research. At first the children were reluctant to try, saying such things as

> "I can't do that."
> "Will you draw me a turkey?"
> "Where's the pattern?"
> "Why can't I just cut out a picture of a turkey and paste it down?"

Once the children realized that I was not going to give them patterns, they became more adventurous. The art teacher had a supply of turkey feathers she used for a painting activity. I borrowed the feathers, and had the children study them under a microscope and make sketches of the feathers' structure before they used them with paint. In addition to the paint, I set out colored pencils, markers, scraps of construction paper, and the "junk box" (found objects such as buttons, sequins, scraps of cloth and ribbon, and small man-made feathers). I encouraged them to rub the feathers between their fingers. I asked the children to tell how the feathers felt. One child said, "I didn't think feathers would feel this way. The big feathers feel stiff, and the little feathers feel soft and fluffy." Then I encouraged the children to experiment with the different art materials that I had set out for them to use. I encouraged them to talk with each other about their ideas.

That year, as the Thanksgiving holiday approached, I saw that the turkeys my students had created were quite different than they had been in previous years. The turkeys no longer were "pattern turkeys." The children went crazy with the materials. When the turkeys were displayed in the corridor by this second-grade classroom, children and adults stopped to admire them individually. Some turkeys were painted with bright colors; some had feathers carefully delineated. Several turkeys were presented on farms; one was on a dining room table, roasted for the holiday. In addition to markers, some children had used paint and actual objects in their presentations. Some children had used feathers to paint their turkeys, a technique they had learned in art class. Several children glued small, colorful feathers onto their turkey bodies. One child had glued popsicle sticks to his paper to fence his turkeys in. That year, my students' turkeys were distinguishable from each other.

A Third-Grade Teacher—Mia Beleos

Even though our curriculum is absorbed in Language Arts and Math skills, I try to integrate art inside the topic. One example was the weather unit. The children read books about tornadoes, graphed storms, charted and plotted storm paths, wrote feeling poems, drew night scenes, and used stormy vocabulary and adjectives to describe such a disaster.

On a more challenging level, students were asked to create a tornado of their own on paper. After a scientific experiment demonstrating the mixture of warm and cool air forming a whirlwind, the key part to illustrating this concept depended on their background art knowledge of warm versus cool colors. In art class, children chose reds, oranges, and yellows for warm air. They drew funnel clouds of warm air spiraling into cool blues, greens, and grays. Having them verbalize the color combustion symbolizing the real-life tornado process called for meaningful transfer of the entire concept. Other art-embedded lessons included linking geometry (symmetry) and spatial sense to technical design and linking the language skill of comparison/contrast to reading as well as to paintings, sculpture, and their own artwork.

The better you internalize both curriculum objectives, the better a classroom teacher and an art specialist can integrate, which makes it more fun and meaningful for the children to remember in life.

The Art Specialist—Diane English

Working with the third-grade teacher is something that I enjoy doing. I find it easiest first to learn what she is focusing on in the classroom and then to find a way to either present the same information through visual art or use art as a vehicle to present new information. By looking through the materials used in the classroom (basal and other texts and visual aids), I could make choices about the type of art the students would be creating. I also used the South Carolina Visual and Performing Arts Curriculum Standards to create lessons that would touch on the four components: Aesthetic Perception, Creative Expression, Visual Arts Heritage, and Aesthetic Valuing. By using the same focus as the classroom (in this case, weather), students could and did use new vocabulary and concepts outside the regular classroom. I think this gave the students a deeper understanding of the subject.

Overall, the collaboration between the classroom teacher and me did not take an extraordinary amount of time or effort. Yes, it was a change; but I think it was a very beneficial change for the students and us. We had a better understanding of what was being taught in our respective rooms and how it was being taught, and the students experienced learning that was not isolated in our classrooms.

REFLECTIONS FROM TWO PRINCIPALS

The First Principal—Stephen Ward

As a result of observing one teacher's instruction and the progress of her students over the past 2 years, I have a better understanding of chil-

dren with developmental delays. In past years, I have seen children identified for the 4-year-old program (this program is for children from low-
socioeconomic backgrounds) who make little progress and continue to have
delays throughout their elementary education. However, with this project,
I have seen kids come into the program and flourish. It's like a butterfly
that comes out of a cocoon. By the end of the school year, the children are
demonstrating competencies equal to and sometimes even surpassing those
of children in the 5-year-old program. Each year, the number of children
meeting with success continues to increase. With the emphasis on art, I
have seen how children can use language to describe, compare and contrast, and elaborate on details. It also encourages the child even to be self-
correcting and take risks. As a result of this program, my whole perspective
of children with developmental delays has changed by increasing my ex-
pectations of the child and the teacher.

The teacher's displays of the children's work have made our school
a more inviting place. The displays and the children's work were very creative. While serving as documentation for the children's level of success,
the displays also served as a type of professional development for other
teachers. The displays showed the children's progress, growth, and what
they had been learning (see Figure 8.4). They really boosted the children's
self-concept. The students would take your hand and lead you to their work.
Parents frequently gathered around the displays. The displays often created an interest among the older students, who then wanted to visit the
4-year-old classroom.

With the emphasis on accountability in each subject area, we have
learned the limitations of teaching content in isolation. In addition, teaching in isolation does not foster learning and mastery because often the learning isn't associated with meaning in the child's life experiences. This teacher
mastered the technique of teaching a transdisciplinary curriculum. She
exhibited the principles of Vygotsky in her daily instruction with the children. By using art as the medium for expression, this teacher began the
process of developing phonemic awareness, letter recognition, and the
writing process. The art experience was the beginning of how children make
language and how they give meaning to it. Through art, the teacher and
the student explored many concepts.

The Second Principal—Larry Doggett

I think the thing I'm impressed with is that a lot of the kids in our
school may have had some difficulty in learning some of the skills that
we're trying to teach. Normally we talk about accommodating the different modalities of learning; but when you bring art into it, it brings greater
levels of deeper thinking. I think art touches another level of brain functioning that we really hadn't thought about. It helps the students learn
more than we would have thought they could. I've been really impressed
with how art brings the other subjects alive, and how the learning trans-

FIGURE 8.4 The hall corridor has high visibility for a teacher's documentation panel. It is as aesthetically pleasing as it is educative.

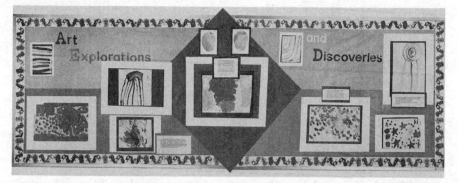

fers, and how art makes it real. Not only have the students seen it before, but they recognize it, and they are much more aware of it. Higher order thinking skills are naturally developed when the children start seeing the connections, and they provide transfer in other subjects—like geometric shapes in math and art and in the environment. Art is a natural phenomenon of existence. It seems that this transfer occurs when the children see the artist in themselves.

I'd like to see a plan to get art more integrated into the school, perhaps to include the writing specialist. Art helps the children get more excited about their writing. I think there are a lot of students that we don't reach right now as well as we could by having a more integrated approach such as I have observed in some classrooms.

REFLECTIONS FROM TEACHER EDUCATORS

An Art Educator—Margaret Johnson

As an art educator, I have been very cautious about encouraging elementary classroom teachers to incorporate more art into their curriculum. I feared that the meaningful instruction in art, unless provided by certified art specialists, would be misguided and watered-down, counter to the substantive, discipline-based art education endorsed by our national professional association.

At the same time, I have been concerned that visual art, taught solely by the art specialist, is seldom truly integrated into the child's understanding of his world. I have long felt that students do not have enough time or even the occasion to apply what they have learned from their art specialists to experiences and ideas that really interest them. Students make "school art" in art class; they learn art concepts separated from their other school learning; they learn skills in isolation from daily school experiences. This need not be the case.

Several years ago, before beginning this project, I realized the power of art to express the child's construction of knowledge in an early childhood classroom. I was walking down the early childhood corridor of an elementary school on my way to visit a student teacher. All too often in the past, I had seen on the corridor walls of elementary schools the results of assignments for which I had little regard: the cute, all-alike bunnies or turkeys, or worse, those dreaded mimeographed images that children must color. On the other hand, on the walls near the art room, I would see the results of recent art lessons with the art specialist. As an art educator for 28 years, I always liked to guess the nature of the art lessons I was seeing on school walls, the artistic skills and aesthetic concepts being addressed through art instruction.

But this time I was perplexed. I saw a wall of 4- and 5-year-old artwork, beautifully and powerfully expressed, about farms and farm life for which I could not guess the art assignment. I saw artworks on papers of individual sizes and shapes, with a variety of media used: markers, watercolors, collage materials of all sorts. I saw, in sum, wonderfully creative, and often ingenious, constructions and representations of the children's ideas. I realized the import of what I saw on those walls, introduced myself to the early childhood teacher, and thus began a wonderful opportunity to collaborate in this venture.

As a result of this project, I have witnessed many positive benefits to collaboration of early childhood teachers and visual arts specialists. Art educators who are certified for K–12 may know little about young children, but they are asked to include preschool and kindergarten children in their teaching schedules. Thus, art and early childhood educators may not have a common language with which to communicate, or even time in the school week to share background knowledge and ideas. Clearly, with our collaborative research project we demonstrated how early childhood teachers could use key art ideas, typical classroom art media, and simple artistic processes in their daily teaching.

An Early Childhood Educator—Rosemary Althouse

From the beginning of my involvement in this research project, I had no doubt that art could be integrated into the curriculum. I also felt that Vygotsky's theory of social interaction and language development was a natural way to integrate subject matter areas. Teachers could use the concept of the ZPD to plan experiences for children, and they could use dynamic assessment as one way to assess learning.

I was not surprised that art could be integrated into the curriculum; but I was surprised at some of the interesting ways in which teachers integrated subject matter. For example, children drew the weather conditions for a given day rather than just writing them on a chart. The teacher asked children to research facts about their city and then to show what they had learned using some form of art media. Children of all ages, 4–8, were anxious to become involved in using art media. They also loved the discovery table where they could play with the materials and talk about the things that they found out. They constantly went back and forth from the art table to the discovery table, the discovery table to the art table. They even made suggestions to the teachers of how they might use art to express what they were learning, suggestions such as "Oh, let's draw a picture about that," or "Hey, we could do a collage and show how this can be done instead of just talking about it."

The children's ability to use art talk surprised me. I did not think that they would involve art talk so readily into the activities that they were doing, but I heard them talk about their use of design and color, line, shades and tints, and about all kinds of shapes, geometric shapes and free form shapes. The children talked not only to the teachers but to each other. Prior to doing this study, I had listened in three different classrooms to children's conversations as they engaged in their artwork. I did not overhear them talking to each other about the art that they were doing. Sometimes they made comments to each other about color; but other than that, I didn't find them engaged in a cooperative conversation about working with the materials. However, in this study I heard a great deal of conversation about the artwork as the children worked. These conversations are recorded in this book.

It was especially gratifying to me to find that art experiences encouraged children's use of vocabulary and their interest in all subject matter areas. They were delighted to express their findings in art and to share their pictures with each other. They began to use language that showed that they understood the artwork they saw. They knew something about the artists. They recognized an art reproduction when they saw it. They made comments such as "That looks like a Matisse," and "Oh, did Monet paint that?" They recognized certain characteristics of individual artists, and it was interesting that several of them commented on Van Gogh's use of yellow and Matisse's use of red in their artwork. They enjoyed comparing the artwork of book illustrators. They knew right away, for example, that Robert McCluskey or Eric Carle or Maurice Sendak had illustrated a certain book. This encouraged them to make pictures for their own books. Overall, these children were interested in art media, and the use of art media. They were anxious to talk about their art with each other, visitors to the room, school staff members, and the principal. The teachers in the study became increasingly skilled at using art talk with the children. They knew how to ask questions that encouraged problem solving and creativity. We hope this book will encourage teachers who read it to try art talk with children as they integrate art into their curriculum.

Appendix A
Children's Art Development

Our perspective on children's art development, as incorporated into our study, was that of creative thinking. In our research we asked the teachers to use a rating scale when they reviewed the artwork in their students' portfolios (see Figure A.1). There are 10 items on the scale: 5 items relate to creative thinking, 3 items relate to cognitive thinking, and 2 items relate to aesthetic thinking; yet, all 10 items relate to artistic thinking in general.

The first 6 items on the scale can be observed in individual pieces of the child's artwork: repleteness, elaboration, originality, composition, expression, and fluency. The remaining 4 characteristics would typically be observed in the child's artistic behavior over time: flexibility, problem solving, transfer of artistic knowledge and skills, and use of art language to discuss work.

CREATIVE THINKING IN ART

According to Efland (1990), there was a post-Sputnik argument that art should be valued in education for its ability to encourage the development of creative problem solving skills long before other areas of education can do so. Efland wrote further that Lowenfeld (1958)

> believed that the purpose of art is to develop creativity and that the promise it could transfer to other spheres of human activity can be seen in the fact that creativity is the same in all areas. He cited the work of J. P. Guilford who speculated that there are specific traits possessed by creative individuals in all fields. (Efland, 1990, p. 237)

In discussing Guilford's (1977) work, Schirrmacher (1997) characterizes divergent or creative thinking with four mental qualities: fluency, flexibility, originality, and elaboration. In the Art Portfolio Assessment Scale, we included these four qualities, along with a fifth, an inclination toward and enjoyment of general creative problem solving itself.

Fluency can be defined as a confident, skillful use of an art medium and/or tools. Fluency is exhibited in the extent to which a child's artwork reflects control, confidence, and, if possible, choice in the art medium and/or tools used. For example, the child has varied the pressure of crayon on paper to achieve various effects of lighter or darker grass or trees; or the child has selected particular media for their expressive qualities, as when oil pastels are chosen over crayons for their more intense coloring capabilities.

FIGURE A.1 Art Portfolio Assessment Scale.

Child's Name _____   Date _____

Study Theme _____

Qualities Exhibited in Child's Artwork			RATING SCALE			
	(low)				(high)	
Repleteness (details)	1	2	3	4	5	N/A
Elaboration (details)	1	2	3	4	5	N/A
Originality	1	2	3	4	5	N/A
Composition	1	2	3	4	5	N/A
Expression	1	2	3	4	5	N/A
Fluency	1	2	3	4	5	N/A
Characteristics of Child Observed						
Flexibility	1	2	3	4	5	N/A
Problem solving	1	2	3	4	5	N/A
Transfer of artistic knowledge and skills	1	2	3	4	5	N/A
Use of art language to discuss work	1	2	3	4	5	N/A

Flexibility, according to Schirrmacher, is "the ability to mentally push boundaries" (1997, p. 22). Flexible artists do not become discouraged by "accidents of media"; they can use an ink smudge that blurred as an artistic device, for example, to show motion lines. Teachers are encouraged to emphasize that what may seem like an accident can actually become a new idea—a drop of paint or a line awry can lead the artist to a richer expression.

Originality is a third quality of divergent or creative thinking. This quality marks artwork that is unique, unusual, or unexpected; that demonstrates imaginative thinking, with schemas and environments that are fresh and individual; and that exhibits personal, not stereotypical, symbols to represent ideas. Artistic originality is hindered when children are given coloring books or dittoed worksheets with cute and common images to color. Artistic originality is encouraged when children are given hands-on experience with objects and ideas, as with field trips, discovery tables, and many opportunities to draw (see Smith et al., 1998).

Elaboration is evidenced when children add many details to their artwork. Through elaboration, visual complexity is created. Elaboration indicates an extensive understanding of the characteristics of the objects, images, or events represented (Harris, 1963), and an embellishment of the ordinary or mundane into a rich artistic expression. An elaborate rendering of a flower, for example, would include pistils and/or stamens, along with the petals, and leaves particular to its kind.

The fifth quality, *creative problem solving*, is seen when a child demonstrates an inclination toward, and enjoyment of, creative problem solving in general. Such a child seeks and solves creative problems and devises them even where they did not exist. For example, a child may not be challenged by a particular open-ended assignment such as illustrating a group of monsters from Sendak's *Where the Wild Things Are* (1963), preferring instead to draw his monsters advancing toward the reader, and ranging in size from large (nearer) and small (farther away).

COGNITIVE THINKING IN ART

The three items on the Art Portfolio Assessment Scale that relate to cognitive thinking are repleteness, transfer of artistic knowledge and skills, and use of art language to discuss work. *Repleteness* is similar to elaboration, as both qualities attend to details. However, repleteness indicates knowledge of the subject, theme, or idea portrayed or expressed in the artwork, while elaboration demonstrates knowledge of particular details of individual subjects represented. For example, with regard to repleteness, a child's artwork will show a variety of flowers in a garden, reflecting a broad knowledge in general; while elaboration within the child's work demonstrates a knowledge of particular flowers by including many details, such as the parts of the particular flower, its leaf formation, and its colors.

Transfer of artistic knowledge and skills is evidenced when the child uses previous knowledge about materials, tools, and concepts in a new or different situation. For example, a child might apply what she knows about using modeling clay to hypothesize how Degas created his sculptures of ballerinas. She has experienced the process of modeling forms in clay; therefore she can transfer this experiential knowledge to a broader consideration of the concept outside of herself. She can imaginatively re-create the Degas sculpture through her prior experience with clay, and can demonstrate her understanding of the clay process if she guesses that Degas created his ballerina by shaping her with clay.

The *use of art language to discuss art work* would be evident as a child talks with her peers or adults about her own and others' work. Extending the example above, the child would use art vocabulary such as *sculpture* or *form*; she might include some reference to the process of modeling or sculpting, perhaps mentioning how difficult it is to balance a heavier form, such as a body, on top of thinner coils or legs. She may recall the name of a sculptor she knows or whose work she has seen in reproductions or museums.

AESTHETIC THINKING

The third broad category of consideration in artistic development is the aesthetic category. Although terms in the preceding two categories may also be said to relate to aesthetic qualities, composition and expression are central to a consideration of the artworks themselves; they are aesthetic qualities inherent in the artworks.

Composition is the arrangement of the elements of design, the organization of the elements of the artwork in terms of principles such as unity, balance, and harmony. Early in a child's artistic development, composition appears to be intuitive; later, composition is taught in art instruction. For example, a child's painting of flowers has them arranged in an intuitively balanced manner (most often symmetrical); colors may be used intuitively for emphasis or pattern. The element of space or depth may be present through the use of overlapping, placement, or relative size (to indicate depth, larger trees are nearer the viewer, with smaller trees placed closer to the horizon line). While balance and color may be intuitively applied in a young child's composition, appropriate use of space to show depth is usually the result of instruction.

Expression is the extent to which the artwork shows feelings or emotional qualities. The child's artwork presents the subject in an affective manner. The viewer can "feel" the fuzzy petals of the flower; the shimmering heat of the sun; the soft, curving edge of the butterfly wing; the jagged, sharp teeth in the open jaws of the shark.

AESTHETIC THINKING AND ART TALK

Aesthetic thinking forms the foundation of criticism and aesthetics, areas of art study that are developed in focused instruction in art classes after the early childhood years. Talking about art in the context of art experience is the means to aesthetic thinking. Art talk (see Appendix B) provides the vocabulary and knowledge necessary for the young artist to communicate artistic ideas. For example, the early childhood teacher can talk with the young child about his artwork, not only in terms of the subject, theme, or objects identified within the work, but also about the artwork's composition and its expressive qualities. And, importantly, such talk can take place within the context of the art-making experience and the sharing of the work with others.

When early childhood teachers engage in art talk with their students, they lay the foundation for a lifetime of dialogue in the art world. As one art teacher observed, young children who have engaged in art talk with their classroom teachers come into the school's formal art classes with an "art readiness" not unlike the readiness that can result from their other early training.

Appendix B
Art Talk: Language of Art

Art talk for the young child includes references to the child's interest in media and tools; the expressive quality of his marks, ideas, feelings, efforts, and inventiveness; and an understanding of the basic elements and principles of design

The elements of design include line, color, shape/form, texture, and space. Found in nature, art, and the man-made environment, these elements are combined to create the principles of design: balance, pattern (repetition/rhythm), emphasis, proportion, unity/variety, and movement. Elements and principles are used to create compositions. Often, elements and principles of design are used intuitively by young children. Elements and principles are taught in art classes, when lessons focus on selected elements or principles in art practice. In the following sections we define the terms of art talk and provide selected examples of its use (see Figure B.1 for an Art Talk Checklist).

The Art Talk Checklist may be used to chart the growth of students' artistic vocabulary and concepts. The checklist focuses on the language of many, but not all, of the elements and one principle of design, used in talking with young children about artwork, and on the children's spontaneous talk about art.

THE LANGUAGE OF THE ELEMENTS OF DESIGN

Line is usually considered to be a continuous mark on a surface, although it may just be implied when our eyes move from point to point in a composition. Lines have directionality: horizontal, vertical, and diagonal. Lines may be straight or curved, fat or thin, long or short. Young children usually begin their art development with sweeping horizontal lines on a surface; later, their motor control develops so that they can make vertical, then circular, lines. Five-year-old Alex used two single, long straight lines to indicate legs on his drawing of himself. His teacher called his attention to the vertical, sturdy legs he drew giving the impression of "standing tall"; she thereby helped him to connect his drawn visual symbols with expressive verbal language.

Color can be used realistically, or for expressive, symbolic, or even decorative purposes. There are three key characteristics of color: hue, value, and intensity.

1. *Hue* is the color name, such as red or red-violet. There are three primary hues: red, blue, and yellow; three secondary hues: orange, violet, and green; and six tertiary hues: red-violet and red-orange, blue-violet and blue-green, yellow-orange and yellow-green.

FIGURE B.1 Art Talk Checklist.

Child's Name_____   **Date** _____

COLOR

Hue

Names *primary* colors

_____ red

_____ blue

_____ yellow

Names *secondary* colors

_____ green

_____ violet (purple)

_____ orange

Mixes primary colors to make secondary colors

_____ green

_____ violet (purple)

_____ orange

And can state how they are made

_____ green

_____ violet (purple)

_____ orange

Uses the words *hue* and *color* interchangeably _____

Value

Names *neutral* colors

_____ white

_____ black

_____ brown

_____ gray

Mixes black with color to make a *shade*   _____

States that adding black to a color makes it darker   _____

Mixes white with a color to make a *tint*   _____

States that adding white to a color makes it lighter   _____

Recognizes a range of a hue's value in artwork   _____

Uses a range of a hue's value in his or her artwork   _____

Comments:

LINE

Uses various lines in artwork:

_____ straight

_____ curved

_____ zigzag

_____ horizontal

_____ vertical

_____ diagonal

Describes lines as:

_____ straight

_____ curved

_____ zigzag

_____ horizontal

_____ vertical

_____ diagonal

(continued)

FIGURE B.1 (*continued*)

SHAPE

Uses various shapes in artwork: Names shapes as:

_____ geometric   _____ geometric

_____ circle   _____ circle

_____ square   _____ square

_____ rectangle   _____ rectangle

_____ triangle   _____ triangle

_____ oval   _____ oval

_____ diamond   _____ diamond

_____ organic (natural)   _____ organic (natural)

_____ free-form   _____ free-form

COMPOSITION

Uses *balance* in artwork: Identifies *balance* in artwork:

_____ symmetrical   _____ symmetrical

_____ radial   _____ radial

_____ asymmetrical or overall   _____ asymmetrical or overall

CHILD TALKS ABOUT ART

Without prompting, describes his/her artwork to adults _____

Talks about lines   _____   Comments: _____

Talks about shapes   _____   Comments: _____

Talks about colors   _____   Comments: _____

Talks about content   _____   Comments: _____

Tells a story about the artwork _____   Comments: _____

Talks about discoveries during art exploration _____

Talks about specific media used in artwork (e.g., paints) _____

Talks about special techniques used in artwork _____

Uses planning with artwork:

_____ verbalizes plans   _____ plans on paper   Comments:_____

Appears to contemplate artwork _____   Comments: _____

Shows and describes artwork to children ("Look at my picture" or "I made green") _____

Comments: _____

Makes suggestions to other children ("Draw a tree here" or "Wash your brush first") _____

Comments: _____

2. *Value* is the relative lightness or darkness of a hue; tints and shades are produced when white (tints) or black (shades) is added to a hue.
3. *Intensity* is varied by adding a hue's complement (its opposite on the color wheel) to the hue; for example, red becomes duller, less intense when green is added to it.

Young children start out using color for no purpose other than utility: a red marker within reach is chosen simply because it is there, it is handy. When a range of colors are presented, young children often select and use them in a sequential fashion, more to discover what each one looks like it seems, than to choose them with an artistic purpose in mind: realistic, expressive, or decorative.

Maria makes rainbows from the different colors in the crayon box, arranging them sequentially, hue arching over hue. When Maria's teacher wants her to explore value, she asks her to study a painting by Monet and point out which blues are lighter, which darker. Next, she has Maria explore tints and shades in her own painting; she limits her color choices to one hue with white and black and asks her to mix her own tints and shades.

After some experience with color media, young children use color for its expressive qualities, enjoying color intensity for itself. As they grow older, they usually want to use color for realistic purposes. Symbolic use of color is taught in later grades.

Shape and *form* are two terms to describe the contours of enclosed spaces in art. Shape is used to refer to two-dimensional works such as drawings and paintings, and form for three-dimensional pieces such as sculpture and architecture. Shapes and forms may be described as *geometric, organic* or *free-form.* Five-year-old Damien pointed out and counted all the circle shapes in a Miró painting. He cut three circles from white paper to create a snowman for his winter scene. Shortly after 7-year-old Sally had seen several of Matisse's cut-paper collages, she was inspired to cut free-form spiral shapes to add to her own collage of found materials. When she hung one of these shapes in the air, she discovered that she had made a three-dimensional form that moved in a breeze.

Texture is the feeling of the surface quality. It can be rough (like a sandpaper alphabet letter) or soft (like a chalk drawing); it can be furry (as in a piece of material) or slick (as in manipulating finger paint); it can be real (like a piece of tree bark glued in a collage) or visual (like the implied bark of a tree trunk drawn with crayons). Five-year-old Nakeesha made a new discovery when she was outdoors painting with her class. She gave actual texture to her outdoor painting when she mixed dirt and sand in with the paint. Nakeesha's teacher extended this learning by showing her the artwork of Vincent van Gogh and discussing how he used *impasto,* paint thickly applied, with brush strokes making actual textures in the paint.

Wanting to make a picture of his dog more realistic, 6-year-old Maurice combined real and visual texture in his artwork. When he drew himself standing by his dog, he colored his own clothing with markers, and then glued some hair he had clipped from his dog onto the dog in his drawing.

Space is created as an illusion in a two-dimensional format. A three-dimensional form—a sculpture for example—has actual space in its dimensionality: width, height, and depth. Young children learn to create three-dimensional space by several means: overlapping, scale, and placement of shapes; atmospheric perspective is obtained through color.

As children grow beyond the early childhood years, they often become dissatisfied with their own drawings when they compare them to "how things really look." Landscapes may look flat and human figures appear out of proportion when children compare their own artwork with what they see around them. Sometimes young children intuitively grasp elementary principles of showing depth: overlapping, relative size, and color differences. More often, though, one-point perspective is a principle taught at the upper elementary level, or when children show an interest in the concept with regard to their own work.

Eight-year-old Lee discovered that when he overlapped shapes, one appeared to be in front of the other. Next, his teacher took him outdoors to help him see that shrubs look larger when they are nearer the viewer, smaller when they are in the distance. She showed him how to place the larger, nearer shapes toward the bottom, or foreground, of his paper, and to place the smaller shapes farther up on the paper so that they would appear to be farther back.

Next, the teacher showed Lee several reproductions of landscape paintings by European and American artists that employed the technique of *atmospheric perspective*. Lee saw that the artists used brighter, more intense colors in the foregrounds, with grayer, duller colors in the backgrounds. Although the term *atmospheric perspective* was beyond Lee's cognitive developmental level, his visual grasp of the principle that brighter colors stand out while duller colors recede, helped him show depth in his later two-dimensional artwork.

THE LANGUAGE OF THE PRINCIPLES OF DESIGN

Balance may be symmetrical, radial, or overall. Six-year-old Dinah unconsciously uses symmetrical balance in her drawing when she adds flowers to the right of her tree to complement those to the left of her tree. She uses radial balance when she draws the petals of a daisy extending from its center in the middle of her paper to its edges. She uses overall balance when she creates a composition of hearts covering her paper in wallpaper fashion. Dinah is taught the term *balance* when her teacher points out to her the symmetry of the flowers to the right and left of her tree, and continues to instruct about symmetry as she looks at a photograph of a butterfly, or shows Dinah how to put paint in the middle of her paper and fold it in half to create a symmetrical shape in paint.

Pattern (*repetition* and *rhythm*) is created when a particular shape, color, or motif is repeated in a rhythmic manner. Patterns provide harmonious or decorative effects in works of art. They enhance and embellish surfaces of artworks as well as their content.

Rachel's teacher drew her attention to patterns in nature, showing her how leaves grow in a systematic, geometric arrangement on tree branches; how some leaves grow in pairs opposite each other on the branch, growing closer together as they approach the end of the branch; and how other leaves grow in a spiral fashion along their stalks.

Proportion (*scale*) involves relationships of sizes, one to another, much as Lee learned when his teacher helped him see how to show depth in a drawing by varying the sizes of his shrubs, large to small. Proportions of faces and figures can be taught when a child shows interest in doing so; but an understanding of proportion develops as the child grows. Children begin their drawing of faces and figures in a schematic manner, with many details omitted and the most important features exaggerated.

Seven-year-old Carlos became interested in proportion after an older sibling pointed out that the heads he drew on his people were much too large for their bodies. When he asked his teacher for help in drawing "better" figures, she showed him how to measure six head lengths for the height of a child's body, and how long to make the arms: with his elbows reaching his waist, and his own fingertips extending to about a hand's length on the tops of his legs.

When 5-year-old Patty proudly showed her teacher a pizza she had drawn, the teacher asked her if she planned to cut it into pieces for her family. "How many pieces of pizza will you need for your family?" Patty answered, "Five, but Daddy will eat two pieces." After Patty had figured that she would need to cut her pizza into six slices, her teacher helped her to do so. When some of the slices turned out to be larger than others, Patty specified who would get which piece, and the teacher suggested that Patty draw each person's favorite toppings on their special slices.

Emphasis is a way artists create a center of interest or focal point in their artwork using spots of bright colors, particular subject matter, texture or pattern, lights and darks (value). The use of contrast in various other design elements can create emphasis, such as when the artist contrasts warm colors with cool colors, rough textures in one area of an otherwise smooth artwork, and highlights on an otherwise dark image.

Four-year-old Latoya intuitively used emphasis in her collage of cut and torn paper. She selected a square of shiny gold foil to glue in the center paper doily on her Valentine card for her mother. She added a ring of glitter glue around the edge of the doily as well, drawing attention to the scalloped edge, as if to tell us how important the doily was in her work. Latoya's teacher seized a "teachable moment" when Latoya showed her the card, relating emphasis in art to emphasis in talking, as when one says a word or phrase louder than the rest of the sentence, drawing attention to it.

Unity and variety are artists' techniques that maintain the viewer's interest in works of art. A unified artwork seems harmonious; nothing should be added or removed. Variety adds interest to a unified work through size and color differences.

Seven-year-old Rose's teacher notes how she unifies her chalk drawing of a flower garden by repeatedly using circular shapes in the flowers, by grouping her flowers together in a circular garden, and by using the color yellow in the flowers, in the sun, and in the hair of the little girl. She uses the word *unity* with Rose with examples of how it works in her drawing. She introduces the art concept of "color family" to Rose and shows her how she harmonizes her colors further by limiting her colors primarily to the warm color family (yellow, orange, reds, and their mixed variations). Yet Rose uses variety in her drawing where she added green leaves and stems to her daffodils, and several red tulips in the garden. The contrast in colors is enhanced with value differences as well, when Rose mixes white in some of her colors to produce tints.

Movement in a work of art is generally seen in two ways: the illusion of movement in a composition, or the actual movement of our eyes as we view the work. For example, a figure with arms and legs bent can show running or jumping. The illusion of movement is enhanced in cartoon drawings with action lines extending from moving limbs or dust balls by shuffling feet. Movement can be less obvious though, when we sense movement through a repetition of flowing lines or of shapes that progress large to small across the composition. When a particularly bright or intense color is placed in certain places of the composition, we find that it moves our eyes around the composition drawing our attention to certain parts of the work.

Eight-year-old Sam enjoys making action drawings: sports, armies, construction, and traffic. His older brother Tom has recently become interested in illustration and cartooning. One evening, Tom and Sam looked at several comic books together. They especially enjoyed action hero figures. They "read" the visuals before they read the bubble text. They discovered the effects of drawing movement lines in a drawing. Sam's next drawings included action lines beside the baseball being thrown by him to his friend, with action lines and dust balls behind a previously static truck on a highway.

ART TALK AND ART APPRECIATION

Art talk is not limited to vocabulary: It also includes acquaintance with different media and processes, and a continuing interest in, and enjoyment of, the arts. All educators, whether early childhood or art specialists, and other adults in children's lives are encouraged to continue to learn about art and artists, visit museums and galleries, and invite artists into the schools. To be most effective in art talk, they need to continue to enjoy experiences with art.

SUGGESTIONS FOR TALKING WITH CHILDREN ABOUT THEIR ART

How teachers use art talk with children and how they encourage them to share art talk determines how well the children express themselves with art media. The following are suggestions for teachers to use to facilitate art expression. They summarize points made throughout this book.

1. *Use correct art terms.* The teacher may say, "You made a secondary color." "How did you make that tint?" "I see you drew straight lines, zigzag lines, and diagonal lines." "Can you point out some free-form shapes in your collage?"

2. *Encourage children to reflect on their art experiences.* Keep art portfolios and ask questions about their work. "Which picture do you like best?" "Which one did you work on the hardest?" When a child spends several days on a painting, talk to the child about the changes you observe each day.

3. *Ask convergent questions.* "What color did you make?" "What geometric shape is this?" "What artist did you say the painting reminded you of?"

4. *Ask divergent questions.* "What are some materials you could use in your farm picture?" "What ideas do you have about Monet's painting?"

5. *Focus children's attention on the way they use art media.* "I see you are drawing circles with the blue marker." "How did you make the sides so high on your clay cup?" "How did you turn your clay into a ball?"

6. *Label the child's actions.* "You are pouring blue paint into red paint. What color did you make?" "You are making a shade with the black paint."

7. *Introduce new art concepts with actions.* Model art process as you present a concept. The teacher talks out loud: "Oh dear, I want a lighter tint of blue for my sky. Here, I'll add more white to my paint."

8. *Verbalize a problem and help children find a solution.* A child becomes frustrated using a white crayon on white paper, and the teacher asks, "I wonder if we could see your drawing better if we use a different color crayon. What other colors could you use to help you see the lines?"

9. *Encourage children to discuss and arrive at solutions to art problems.* "We need windows for our cardboard school bus. Is there anything in this box that we could use?" "Could we use this piece of plastic?" "Is there anything else we need?"

10. *Connect art with other areas of learning.* Children visit a pet store and, as a follow-up activity, use the puppet stage to create their own pet store. They bring stuffed animals from home to sell in their store. They draw and color pictures of animals to decorate their pet store.

11. *Encourage children to talk about their artwork.* The teacher says, "Tell me about this part of your picture." A child answers, "I drew pets—a cat, a gerbil, and a dog." The teacher says, "Tell me more about what is around your picture." The child answers, "I made a border of stars."

12. *Share art experiences.* Listen to what children say to each other about their artwork. Encourage children to describe the processes they used to create a product.

13. *Make sure that children understand art concepts and techniques.* "How did you make green paint?" "What happened to this line? Where does it end?" "How did you use the lines to make this picture interesting?"

14. *Encourage private speech.* A child is talking to himself as he makes a house. He says, "I am going to use this small box to make my house. I am going to make a roof on it. Here is a box I can use." Does the verbalization appear to help the child as he completes his house? Observe the child to determine when the speech becomes internalized.

15. *Give children firsthand experiences to develop concepts and stimulate art expression.* A class went outside to observe the weather, and instead of writing about it, they drew pictures to share with other children.

16. *Encourage children to talk together about their art.* Jaime watched Alex drawing a picture of the gerbils. The teacher said, "Alex, tell Jaime about your picture. How did you make brown paint?"

17. *Talk with children about artists from various cultures and countries.* The teacher showed the children artworks of several well-known artists, including Claude Monet, Romare Bearden, and Georgia O'Keeffe. In this manner the teacher introduced children to a French impressionist artist, an African American artist, and a female American artist.

18. *Refer to children as artists.* Emily constructed several books throughout the year, and she always signed her name at the bottom of each page like a real artist. The teacher commented, "we show how proud we are of our artwork when we sign our pictures like artists do."

19. *Make connections between and among concepts.* Use a Venn diagram to compare works of art. The teacher says to the children, "Look at the painting by Claude Monet and the collage next to it by Henri Matisse. What colors are alike? Do the artists use any of the same shapes? What shapes are alike?"

20. *Give children time to think about art.* Pose questions about art processes and wait for the children to respond. "How did you paint your picture?" "What did you do first?" "How did you make that color?" Reflection is an important part of art process. All artists reflect on their work.

References

Alkema, C. (1971). *Art for the exceptional*. Boulder, CO: Pruett.

Anderson, F. (1978). *Art for all the children: A creative sourcebook for the impaired child*. Springfield, IL: Charles C. Thomas.

Barden, M. (1993). A backward look: From Reggio Emilia to progressive education. In C. Edwards, L. Gandini, & G. Forman (Eds.), *The hundred languages of children: The Reggio Emilia approach to early childhood education* (1st ed., pp. 283–295). Norwood, NJ: Ablex.

Berk, L. E., & Winsler, A. (1995). *Scaffolding children's learning: Vygotsky and early childhood education*. Washington, DC: National Association for the Education of Young Children.

Bodrova, E., & Leong, D. J. (1996). *Tools of the mind: The Vygotskian approach to early childhood education*. Englewood Cliffs, NJ: Prentice-Hall.

Bradley, W. (1968). A preliminary study of the effect of verbalization and personality orientation on art quality. *Studies in Art Education, 9*(2), 31–38.

Bredekamp, S., & Copple, C. (Eds.). (1997). *Developmentally appropriate practice in early childhood programs* (2nd ed.). Washington, DC: National Association for the Education of Young Children [NAEYC].

Brett, J. (1989). *The mitten: A Ukrainian folktale*. New York: Putnam.

Bricker, D., & Woods-Cripe, J. (1995). *An activity-based approach to early intervention* (3rd ed.). Baltimore, MD: Paul H. Brooks.

Bruner, J. (1966). *Studies in cognitive growth: A collaboration at the Center for Cognitive Studies*. NY: Wiley.

Burton, J. (1980a). Beginnings of artistic language. *School Arts, 80*(1), 6–12.

Burton, J. (1980b). The first visual symbols. *School Arts, 80*(2), 60–65.

Cadwell, L. (1997). *Bringing Reggio Emilia home: An innovative approach to early childhood education*. New York: Teachers College Press.

Cohen, D., Stern, K., & Balaban, N. (1997). *Observing and recording the behavior of young children* (4th ed.). New York: Teachers College Press.

Colbert, C., & Taunton, M. (1992). *Developmentally appropriate practices for the visual arts education of young children*. Reston, VA: National Art Education Association [NAEA].

Cromer, J. (1975). The influence of verbal language on aesthetic performance. *Art Education, 28*(2), 14–17.

DeLuise, D. (1990). *Charlie the caterpillar*. New York: Simon & Schuster.

DeVries, R., & Kohlberg, L. (1987). *Programs of early education: The constructivist view*. White Plains, NY: Longman.

Dewey, J. (1980). *Art as experience*. New York: Perigee Books. (Originally published 1934)

Dixon-Krauss, L. (1996). *Vygotsky in the classroom: Mediated literacy instruction and assessment*. White Plains: Longman.

Douglas, N., & Schwartz, J. (1967). Increasing awareness of art ideas of young children through guided experiences with ceramics. *Studies in Art Education, 8*(2), 2–9.

Dubin, E. (1946). The effect of training on the tempo of graphic representations in preschool children. *Journal of Experimental Education, 15*(2), 166–175.

Edwards, C., Gandini, L., & Forman, G. (Eds.). (1998). *The hundred languages of children: The Reggio Emilia approach to early childhood education—advanced reflections* (2nd ed.). Stamford, CT: Ablex.

Efland, A. (1990). *A history of art education: Intellectual and social currents in teaching the visual arts*. New York: Teachers College Press.

Eisner, E. (1990). Implications of artistic intelligences for education. In W. J. Moody (Ed.), *Artistic intelligences: Implications for education* (pp. 31–42). New York: Teachers College Press.

Engle, B. (1995). *Considering children's art: Why and how to value their works*. Washington, DC: National Association for the Education of Young Children.

Forman, G. (1994). *Different media, different languages*. Paper presented at the Study Seminar on the Experience of the Municipal Infant-Toddler Centers and Preprimary Schools of Reggio Emilia (Reggio Emilia, Italy, May 30–June 10, 1994). (Report No. PS 022 558). Washington, DC: U.S. Department of Education, Office of Educational Resources Information Center. (ERIC Document Reproduction Service No. ED 375 932)

Fox, J., & Diffily, D. (2000). Integrating the visual arts—Building young children's knowledge, skills, and confidence. *Dimensions of Early Childhood, 29*(1), 3–10.

Galdone, P., & Peek, M. (1999). *Three little kittens*. New York: Houghton Mifflin.

Gardner, H. (1980). *Artful scribbles: The significance of children's drawings*. New York: Basic Books.

Gardner, H. (1983). *Frames of mind: The theory of multiple intelligences*. New York: Basic Books.

Gardner, H. (1990). *Art education and human development*. Los Angeles: Getty Center for Education in the Arts.

Goldberg, M. (1997). *Arts and learning: An integrated approach to teaching and learning in multicultural and multilingual settings*. New York: Longman.

Guay, D. (1999). A way in: Strategies for art instruction for students with special needs. In A. Nyman & A. Jenkins (Eds.), *Issues and approaches to art for students with special needs*. Reston, VA: National Art Education Association.

Guilford, J. P. (1977). *Way beyond the IQ*. Buffalo, NY: Creative Education Foundation.

Hamblen, K. (1984). "Don't you think some bright colors would improve your painting?" *Art Education, 37*(1), 12–14.

Harris, D. (1963). *Children's drawings as a measure of intellectual maturity*. New York: Harcourt, Brace & World.

Helm, J., Beneke, S., & Steinheimer, K. (1998). *Windows on learning: Documenting young children's work*. New York: Teachers College Press.

Hendrick, J. (1997). *First steps toward teaching the Reggio way*. Upper Saddle River, NJ: Merrill.

Henley, D. (1992). *Exceptional children, exceptional art*. Worcester, MA: Davis.

Hogg, J., & McWhinnie, H. (1968). A pilot research in aesthetic education. *Studies in Art Education, 9*(2), 52–60.

Integrated Curricula Theme Criteria. National School Conference Institute, November 1–5, 1994. Orlando, FL.

Jalongo, M. R., & Stamp, L. N. (1997). *The arts in children's lives: Aesthetic education in early childhood*. Needham Heights, MA: Allyn & Bacon.

Katz, L. (1990). Impressions of Reggio Emilia preschools. *Young Children, 45*(2), 11–12.

Katz, L., & Chard, S. (1996). *Engaging children's minds: The project approach.* Norwood, NJ: Ablex.

Katz, L., & Chard, S. (2000). *Engaging children's minds: The project approach* (2nd ed.). Stamford, CT: Ablex.

Lowenfeld, V. (1958). Current research on creativity. *NEA Journal, 47,* 538–540.

National Art Education Association [NAEA]. (1995). *National Visual Arts Standards.* Reston, VA: Author.

Ringgold, F. (1991). *Tar beach.* New York: Crown.

Rodriguez, S. (1984). *The special artist's handbook.* Palo Alto, CA: Dale Seymour Publications.

Rotner, S., & Kreisler, K. (1996). *Citybook.* Boston: Houghton Mifflin.

Schirrmacher, R. (1997). *Art and creative development for young children* (3rd ed.). Albany, NY: Delmar.

Seefeldt, C. (1995). Art: A serious work. *Young Children, 50*(3), 33–38.

Sendak, M. (1963). *Where the wild things are.* New York: Harper & Row.

Sharp, P. (1976). Aesthetic response in early education. *Art Education, 29*(5), 25–28.

Simpson, J., Delaney, J., Carroll, K., Hamilton, C., Kay, S., Kerlavage, M., & Olson, J. (1998). *Creating meaning through art: Teacher as choice maker.* Upper Saddle River, NJ: Merrill.

Slavin, R. (1994). *Educational psychology: Theory and practice* (5th ed.). Boston: Allyn & Bacon.

Smith, N., & The Drawing Study Group. (1998). *Observation drawing with children.* New York: Teachers College Press.

Sparling, J., & Sparling, M. (1973). How to talk to a scribbler. *Young Children, 28*(4), 333–341.

Taunton, M. (1983). Questioning strategies to encourage young children to talk about art. *Art Education, 36*(4), 40–43.

Thompson, C. (1988). *"I make a mark": The significance of talk in young children's artistic development* (Report No. PS 017 753). Washington, DC: U.S. Department of Education, Office of Educational Resources Information Center. (ERIC Document Reproduction Service No. ED 302 345)

Varnon, D. (1994). In Very Special Arts Education Office, *Start with the arts: A national program of very special arts* (p. 3). Washington, DC: Author.

Venezia, M. (1994). *Jackson Pollock.* Chicago: Children's Press.

Vygotsky, L. (1962). *Thought and language.* (E. Hanfmann & G. Vakar, Eds. and Trans.) Cambridge, MA: MIT Press.

Vygotsky, L. (1971). *The psychology of art.* (Scripta Technica, Inc., Trans.) Cambridge, MA: MIT Press.

Wadsworth, B. J. (1966). *Piaget's theory of cognitive and affective development: Foundations of constructivism* (15th ed.). White Plains, NY: Longman.

Walling, D. (2001). Rethinking visual arts education: A convergence of influences. *Phi Delta Kappan, 82*(8), 626–628, 630–631.

Wilson, B. (1966). The development and testing of an instrument to measure aspective perception of paintings. (Doctoral dissertation, Ohio State University, 1966). *Dissertation Abstracts International, 27,* 2107A.

Wright, S. (1997). Learning how to learn: The arts as core in an emergent curriculum. *Childhood Education, 73*(6), 361–366.

Index

About the Authors

Rosemary Althouse is professor emeritus of early childhood education at Winthrop University, Rock Hill, South Carolina. She is the former director of the Macfeat Early Childhood Laboratory School and the Center of Excellence in Early Childhood Education, both at Winthrop University. In 1988 she received the Distinguished Professor Award from Winthrop University, and upon retirement in 1999, a citation from the State of South Carolina House of Representatives thanking her for a lifetime of service given to the children of South Carolina. She earned a B.S. from the University of Pennsylvania, an M.A. from the State University of Iowa, and a Ph.D. from Florida State University. Dr. Althouse has published numerous articles in professional journals, and is the coauthor of *Science Experiences for Young Children* and the author of *The Young Child: Learning with Understanding, Investigating Science with Young Children*, and *Investigating Mathematics with Young Children*, all published by Teachers College Press.

Margaret H. Johnson began her career as a public school art teacher in New Hampshire, where she taught for 15 years. After completing a doctorate in art education at Florida State University, she taught art education classes at Winthrop University in South Carolina for 14 years. Dr. Johnson has been honored with a number of awards for her teaching and service, including the 1991 Outstanding Junior Professor at Winthrop University and the 1995 National Art Education Association Higher Education Division Art Educator of the Year. She was awarded Winthrop's first Singleton Endowed Professorship in Teacher Education.

In 2001 Dr. Johnson began teaching art criticism and art education in the Art Education Program at the State University of New York (SUNY) in New Paltz, where she has also served as Art Education Program Director. Her publications focus on art criticism in the schools.

Sharon T. Mitchell is currently teaching in the four-year-old program in the public schools of Fort Mill, South Carolina. She earned a B.S. degree in early childhood education from Western Carolina University in 1978 and received a master's degree in reading from Winthrop University in 2001. She has taught children ages 4–9 for the past 20 years. Mitchell received several curriculum grants in instruction from Winthrop University and the Rock Hill School District Foundation, and she has presented at several state and national conferences in education. She lives in Rock Hill, South Carolina, with husband Dan, son Zach, and daughter Kristen. Her hobbies are horseback riding, reading, and spending time with her family.